"Christy Whittlesey has written a must-have guide for anyone seeking to understand and learn what it means to be an ally of the transgender community. She encourages readers to continue to listen, disrupt the system, and be a voice when others can't. It is full of important information like the power of pronouns and the significance of intersectionality. Whittlesey empowers readers to embrace individuals in their workplace, family, and community."

—*Dr Rayna L. Freedman, fifth grade teacher, MassCUE President, and accomplice to the LGBTQIA+ community*

"An impressive introductory guide to being an ally to a person who is transgender or nonbinary. There are helpful tips related to the importance of language, use of listening skills, and normalizing gender-neutral practices in our daily lives. The content of this book ultimately reminds us to be mindful of the humanity of every person we encounter."

—*Latosha Dixon (she/her), Vice-Chair of the Chelmsford Diversity Racial Equity and Inclusion Committee*

"Christy provides information that every parent should know about being a trans or nonbinary ally, including resources on where to find out more. She gets you thinking from a different perspective and shows that trans people just want to be heard, affirmed, and feel safe. Being a trans ally means taking small, everyday actions. We can all think about our environments and consider how we might make them more gender-inclusive."

—*Kathy Sheedy, mother and volunteer for The Ryan Home Project (home for homeless teens)*

"This book unpacks gender diversity by centering the trans voices we hope to become allies for. Through reading these narratives we learn that becoming an ally is moving from ignorance or complicity to a continuum of continual action that affirms and celebrates our trans students, family members, friends, co-workers, and community members. This resource also serves as a user-friendly toolkit with clear techniques for more inclusive allyship. It is a must-read for educators and families alike."

—*Anthony Beatrice, Executive Director for the Arts, Boston Public Schools*

"This is a well-written, well-researched book that is very informative for the general reader, like me. Excellent recommendations for navigating this changing world and being supportive of trans friends and family members."

—*Don M., Boston, MA*

T0046238

of related interest

**Everything You Ever Wanted to Know About
Trans (But Were Afraid to Ask)**
Brynn Tannehill
ISBN 978 1 78592 826 0
eISBN 978 1 78450 956 9

The A–Z of Gender and Sexuality
From Ace to Ze
Morgan Lev Edward Holleb
ISBN 978 1 78592 342 5
eISBN 978 1 78450 663 6

They/Them/Their
A Guide to Nonbinary and Genderqueer Identities
Eris Young
ISBN 978 1 78592 483 5
eISBN 978 1 78450 872 2

The Spectrum of Sex
The Science of Male, Female, and Intersex
Hida Viloria and Maria Nieto, PhD
ISBN 978 1 78775 265 8
eISBN 978 1 78775 266 5

THE BEGINNER'S GUIDE TO BEING A TRANS ALLY

DR. CHRISTY WHITTLESEY

Jessica Kingsley Publishers
London and Philadelphia

First published in Great Britain in 2022 by Jessica Kingsley Publishers
An Hachette Company

3

Copyright © Christy Whittlesey 2022

All rights reserved. No part of this publication may be reproduced, stored
in a retrieval system, or transmitted, in any form or by any means without
the prior written permission of the publisher, nor be otherwise circulated
in any form of binding or cover other than that in which it is published and
without a similar condition being imposed on the subsequent purchaser.

A CIP catalogue record for this title is available from
the British Library and the Library of Congress

ISBN 978 1 78775 783 7
eISBN 978 1 78775 784 4

Printed and bound by CPI Group (UK) Ltd, Croydon, CR0 4YY

Jessica Kingsley Publishers' policy is to use papers that are natural,
renewable and recyclable products and made from wood grown in
sustainable forests. The logging and manufacturing processes are expected
to conform to the environmental regulations of the country of origin.

Jessica Kingsley Publishers
Carmelite House
50 Victoria Embankment
London EC4Y 0DZ

www.jkp.com

To Emma

ACKNOWLEDGMENTS

Special thanks to Dr. Judy Davidson for her mentorship that set me on this path; to all the amazing participants who contributed their time and shared stories and perspectives with me for this book; to my first readers and unwavering supporters Roger Whittlesey and Bernie Bluhm; and to my family, whose love and encouragement have kept me going through 2020 and beyond. Finally, thank you to Andrew James and the team at Jessica Kingsley Publishers for your commitment to diversity and inclusion and for keeping me focused on this project during the pandemic!

CONTENTS

WHAT IS *BEING A TRUE ALLY?*

This is a book about the idea of trans allyship and how people like me—someone who is not transgender—can effectively participate in building a more safe, equitable, and inclusive world for people who are trans and non-binary. Being a true ally is not about labeling oneself as such—it is about continually engaging in learning, listening, and taking action.

Why is this important?

For me, this is about liberation. Trans visual artist Micah Bazant addresses this idea, creating art that engages with social justice movements and inspires us as viewers to "decolonize ourselves from white supremacy, patriarchy, ableism, and the gender binary" (Bazant, n.d.). One of my favorite pieces of theirs is a portrait of Marsha P. ("Pay It No Mind") Johnson, a Black activist and self-identified drag queen who was a noted figure in the Stonewall uprising of 1969; she also worked with her friend Sylvia Rivera to open the first LGBT youth shelter in the U.S., and was deeply involved with the AIDS Coalition to Unleash Power.

Bazant's portrait features Johnson with flowers in her hair against a blue background, with the statement "No Pride for Some of Us Without Liberation for All of Us" prominently featured above her head. Bazant's words in this piece are inspired by Johnson's activism and her message that we should not celebrate while so many are oppressed.

All oppression is linked. When we participate in limiting or excluding others, we diminish the fulfillment of our own humanity. In order to acknowledge and celebrate the diversity that enriches our communities, we need to stand up for one another. Working for liberation for all is important if we are all to benefit from more inclusive and equitable communities. As we seek to be true allies to our trans and nonbinary family members, friends, colleagues, and community members, we must not only educate ourselves and engage with the trans and nonbinary individuals we know in an affirming and respectful way, but also make consistent and deliberate efforts to dismantle systems that cause harm.

The importance of allyship work cannot be underestimated, as while over the past few decades, transgender and nonbinary individuals have become more visible in media and politics, people who do not look or behave in ways that align with traditional gender stereotypes are still often marginalized or attacked. Street harassment is commonplace for people whose appearances do not align with prevailing gender norms (Davis, 2017), and, in fact, violence against trans people has risen over the past few years; the Human Rights Campaign officially recorded more violent deaths of transgender and gender non-conforming people in the U.S. in 2020 than in any year since it began tracking data (Human Rights Campaign, 2020).

On a broader scale, comprehensive validation and protections depend on who is in power, and indeed can be eroded with the stroke of a pen. For example, during one presidential term in the U.S. alone, the administration revoked existing U.S. Department of Justice and Department of Education regulations related to Title IX's guards against sex discrimination, including discrimination linked to gender identity and transgender status (Phillips, 2017). In addition, in 2017 the U.S. President Donald Trump signed an order to ban transgender military recruits from serving in the armed forces, issued an Executive Order instructing the Attorney General to provide guidance to federal agencies related to interpreting religious liberty protections in Federal Law that could have resulted in significant implications for transgender and nonbinary people (The United States Department of Justice, 2017), and also spearheaded a campaign with the Department of Health and Human Services to redefine gender under Title IX as defined by genitalia at birth (Green, Benner, & Pear, 2018). These facts highlight a desperate need for social change in our society, and cisgender (people who are not transgender) allies will be necessary to create lasting change and make our communities safer and more equitable for all.

I am writing this book to contribute to a multitude of existing stories about why striving to ally and actively working to dismantle structures that oppress people benefit us all, and to offer readers guidance in their efforts to be true allies.

Finally, this book is also a fundraiser, as I will be evenly splitting my author royalties with the Gender Reveal Grant and Mutual Aid Program, which provides support to trans people of color.[1]

How Did I Come to this Project?

I come to this project as an educator, a researcher, and someone who strives to ally with folks who are trans and nonbinary. It must be noted that I do not have a lived experience of being transgender, and cannot speak first-hand about being transgender. Rather, I, like you, am striving to educate myself on the most effective ways to create communities that are gender-friendly.

Transgender and nonbinary people are and always have been engaged in social justice work to support their communities and advocate for equity and civil rights. Cisgender people must also engage in these efforts if we are to create lasting change in our communities, our workplaces,

---

[1]   www.genderpodcast.com/grant

and our families. In the words of Nelson Mandela, "To be free is not merely to cast off one's chains, but to live in a way that respects and enhances the freedom of others" (1995, p.385). I have applied my skills as a researcher to attempt to respect and enhance the freedom of others by inspiring cisgender folks to embrace the process of striving towards allyship. As a cisgender person researching and writing about issues related to transgender folks, I also took great care in my research to offer participants as much control as possible, and to center their voices in this work.

In my day job, I am a school arts administrator working with K-12 students. A few years ago, I began to notice a trend in my discussions with students, educators, and educational leaders: increasingly, students were coming out as transgender or nonbinary within their school communities, and the educators charged with creating positive learning environments for these students often had questions about how to support them effectively. Many were unfamiliar with terminology or simply the "right" thing to do in situations that they had not encountered before, and were concerned that they might do the "wrong" thing and unintentionally cause harm to students. I noticed that many well-intentioned teachers and administrators were uninformed at best, and engaging in transphobic behaviors at worst—and observed that the systems that students were navigating in schools were designed by their very nature to be traumatizing for trans youth.

During this period, I was also working toward my Ph.D. in educational research, and upon investigation found that research in this area to help guide educators was scant. As a result, I decided to make this the focus of my dissertation research so that I could design resources for educators to support them in creating more gender-friendly learning environments. Over the course of several months, I spoke with several trans and nonbinary youth who were in high school or who had recently graduated from high school to learn from them about their educational experiences and to ascertain what changes they believed would make schools better places for other trans students.

After completing my dissertation, I incorporated information gleaned from my own research and a deep literature review into my first book, *It's OK to Say "They": Tips for Educator Allies of Trans and Nonbinary Students*. I also began collaborating with school districts to empower them to make shifts in educator practice and educational structures to better meet the needs of a gender-diverse student population.

Every step leads to other questions. In this case, after writing *It's OK to Say "They"*, my questions moved to, "How do we move this discussion beyond the school? Can we improve our insights and decisions in our other community domains?"

To that end, my research for this book involved a number of conversations with nonbinary and transgender adults and people whom they describe as allies to reflect diverse perspectives, stories, and identities, and to look for common themes with regard to trans people's percep-tions of how cisgender people can work toward allyship.

Throughout the book, I center the voices of the research participants, some of whom prefer to share anonymously, and tie in existing studies and work by trans and nonbinary writers and scholars to encourage readers to consider the meaning of allyship, explore further resources, and take action to create a more "gender-friendly" world (Airton, 2018).

Thank you for picking up this book to consider ways to engage in contributing to liberation for all, regardless of gender!

The Participants

Contributors to this book include a range of trans and nonbinary individuals and people who they describe as "allies." All participants consented to have their stories shared for the purposes of publication, and each had the option of being identified with their name or of sharing information privately and being assigned a pseudonym. Participants are listed below in first-name alphabetical order. Those who wish to have their names withheld for the purposes of privacy are identified with a first-name pseudonym.

Bird (they/them): An accountant who is white and identifies as gender-queer, gender-fluid, or nonbinary. Their gender expression varies dramatically in the two times that we speak: for our first meeting, Bird arrives in a hat, an oversized flannel shirt, baggy jeans, hiking boots, and no makeup. The second time we meet, Bird wears a tight black dress, fishnet stockings, a bold cat eye, and green lipstick. For Bird, fluidity in their gender expression is an important part of their identity.

Charles (he/him): A law student at a university and a community outreach worker for trans youth. He is white and has transitioned medically to affirm his gender. He describes himself as "male." Charles knew at a very early age that he was a male, but experienced trauma throughout his school-age years because of transphobic bullying by peers and teachers. Today, he not only excels in his studies, but also speaks in K-12 schools to share his story and encourage students and educators to accept and support diversity.

Chris Talbot-Heindl (they/them): An editor, zinester, fine artist, and graphic and web designer who describes themselves as a trans nonbinary, pansexual, queer, mixed-race person (separated Indigenous, Japanese, and white). They are the publisher of *The Bitchin' Kitsch*, a quarterly art and lit online and printed magazine prioritizing traditionally marginalized creators.

Fernando Zweifach López (they/them): The Executive Director of San Diego LGBT Pride who describes themselves as nonbinary Latinx, Jewish, first-generation U.S. citizen, former homeless youth, and rape survivor. They are a prominent LGBT community leader who has advocated for the rights of LGBT individuals, couples, and families in a variety of positions over many years.

Frankie (he/him): An artist, cat lover, and actor (white) who describes himself as a "trans dude."

Julian (he/him): A white singer, musician, K-Pop dancer, and student who describes himself as a boy who used to identify as gender-fluid.

Maria (she/her): A professional counselor and youth minister, Maria is a white, cisgender, queer parent of four children, two of whom are trans.

Shawna (she/her): A white singer and graduate student, Shawna is described by Julian as an ally.

WHAT IS ALLYSHIP?

What is allyship, anyway? People increasingly use the term "ally" as a label to denote that they care about a particular community traditionally or currently considered oppressed. Sometimes this word serves as an attempt at signaling virtue ("I'm not a bad person"). In terms of gender diversity, some well-meaning cisgender people use the term "ally" when they really mean, "I do not actively engage in what I believe to be transphobic behaviors."

I assert that allyship is much more than simply being polite to the trans people in our communities, and that we need to think about "ally" as a verb rather than a noun. Ally is truly an action word, and striving to ally with people who are trans and nonbinary means continual engagement in educating ourselves, listening to and centering trans voices, and putting effort into dismantling systems that oppress. As Julian, one of my research participants, explains:

> *Allyship is not just being accepting of trans people. It's being*
> *supporting and celebrating. Acceptance is good, it should be*

the starting foundation, but you bet the best allyship goes a little bit above that. And it's so huge to just treat a trans person like you would treat a cis person: a trans boy is just like any other boy, a trans girl is just like any other girl. Hype them up and like make them feel loved. Allyship is supporting, respecting, and centering transness.

Graphic artist Chris Talbot-Heindl covers the concept of allyship and many other topics in a straightforward manner and visually engaging format in their amazing mini-comic *Chrissplains Nonbinary Advocacy to Cisgender People.* They tell me:

Personally, I don't like the word ally or allyship because I think it's lost its edge over time. People claim to be an ally if they don't actively engage in transphobia (knowingly; some of them still do in less blatant ways). I prefer the term accomplice or co-conspirator. They're active terms that imply an active engagement... For me, an accomplice (or co-conspirator) is someone who assists me in navigating the world in a way that is affirming and safe for me. They take their cues from me; they respect and center my needs; they disengage when I ask them to. They do things in community with me instead of guessing my needs from their lens (which will never fully grasp what I am navigating). Also, an accomplice or co-conspirator will be actively engaged in dismantling the structures that harm me to build a more equitable world in which I will no longer need their help, in the way that I explain it should be done.

I really appreciate how Chris frames the concept of true allyship as adopting the role of "accomplice." In contrast to simply being a passive listener offering a sympathetic ear or taking a supportive position from a distance ("I can't believe they did that to you!"), an accomplice will take the lead of trans community members to actively engage in situations to disrupt systems that oppress at home, at work, and in public.

If this seems like a daunting concept, don't worry! You don't need to be an expert on trans issues to be an accomplice. What is important is learning, listening, and engaging—and you are starting this process by reading this book.

The first step on this journey is to familiarize yourself with language so that you feel comfortable engaging in discussions. The following chapter presents some key terminology and approaches to get started.

GETTING COMFORTABLE
WITH LANGUAGE

If you are reading this book, you are actively engaging in learning more about allyship and how we can create safer, more inclusive communities for people who are trans and nonbinary. One component of being a true ally is continually making efforts to educate oneself on issues and language regarding gender diversity. Language is a powerful force, and because of its potential to contribute to oppression or liberation, it is important for us to consider how we use it.

One thing to consider is that language is constantly evolving. This process has been ongoing for centuries, and each year, new words are added to dictionaries as language continues to change. Terminology related to gender is part of the evolution of language, and often the newer words are created by trans and nonbinary people themselves, rather than being ascribed to by dominant groups. This is an important step because this centers trans voices and gives control to the people whom the words are describing.

As Maria, a counselor and parent of two trans children, beautifully states:

> *I think a lot of the problems that trans people encounter have to do with a society who outright rejects them right from the beginning and doesn't make space for them. And language is a way of making space.*

So what are the key terms everyone should know to begin to make this space?

Terminology: The Basics

There are so many different terms involved in talking about gender and sex, and for some people who are not familiar with these terms, engaging in discussions about these topics can be intimidating. When facing an unfamiliar situation, we have a choice: we can use our resources and educate ourselves, or we can withdraw and decide to simply ignore the topic of gender diversity. The good news is that simply becoming familiar with a few key terms can lay a strong foundation for opening the door to further discussions. Being knowledgeable of the basic terms related to gender and sex is important if we are to create gender-friendly communities where all can thrive.

Anxiety about using vocabulary related to gender

diversity is both a common theme in research literature on this topic and something that I encounter regularly when leading discussion groups. Here are some statements people have made to me regarding their discomfort with language:

> I feel like I'm really behind or I missed the discussion, because I'm really weak on understanding the terms.

> I know there's the question of pronouns, and I get really totally tongue-tied because I don't know—is it when someone is nonbinary when the pronoun issue comes, or is it when someone is a lesbian when the pronoun issue comes?

> I don't have the knowledge I need to really approach it in a sensitive way.

If these sentiments resonate with you, don't worry! It is easier to familiarize yourself with the basics than you may think. Here are a few terms to get you started.

Transgender

Transgender, often shortened to "trans," is an umbrella term that refers to anyone whose gender identity (what someone understands is their gender) does not exclusively align with their assigned sex at birth. Note that I use "assigned sex" here; this is because when a doctor looks at an ultrasound or when a baby is born, they assign a sex marker to medical records based on observable physical characteristics; simply put: most often, penis = boy; vagina = girl. (It should be noted that sometimes people are born with a reproductive or sexual anatomy that doesn't fall within the typical definitions of female or male; the term for this is "intersex.")

There are many words that people use to describe their own gender, and this list continues to develop as people discover terms that feel right for them.

Someone who is trans may choose to transition socially, legally, and medically—or not. It is not necessary to take hormones, present in any particular way, or have gender-affirming surgery to be considered trans. Basically, if someone understands themselves to be trans, then they're trans!

The word transgender is an adjective, so we might say, "She is transgender," just like we would say, "She is happy." Transgender is not an adverb, so we would not say, "She is transgendered." Appropriate use in this case would be, "She is a transgender person." Transgender is also not a noun, so we would not say, "That transgender is happy." Appropriate use in this case would be, "That transgender person is happy."

Finally, transgender refers to gender, not sexuality. Just as a person whose gender aligns with their assigned sex at birth can be gay, straight, queer, bisexual, asexual, etc., so can a transgender person. Gender and sexuality are two different things.

Nonbinary

Nonbinary is also an adjective, and is another umbrella term that generally falls within the category of transgender. I am including this term on the "short list" because it is important that we understand and acknowledge that gender does not need to be binary. For some people, this is a challenging idea, but nonbinary genders are valid!

It's easy to understand why this concept might be new to some of us; after all, many people were raised with the idea that there is a physical sex binary (penis/vagina) and a gender binary (male/female). But this idea of a strict binary in relation to sex or gender excludes people who do not neatly fit into these categories, including people who are intersex (those with differences in external sex traits or internal anatomy) or people who are nonbinary.

Simply put, if someone's gender falls within a binary category, they identify as male or female 100% of the time, and just as a cisgender person who identifies as male or female has a binary gender, a transgender person who identifies as male or female also has a binary gender. If someone does not identify with a male or female gender all of the time, they are nonbinary.

Please note that there are other terms that relate to nonbinary genders, such as gender-queer or gender-fluid (and many more). It is up to each person to find the term that fits their gender best.

Still confused? Bird described their gender to me in this way:

I describe it usually as a chameleon effect—depending on what I feel as I wake up in the morning is how I try to present myself, at least in terms of gender expression. And usually that relates to how I'm feeling in my mind. If I'm like, "Oh, I'm feeling really pretty today, I'm gonna wear a skirt," I'll do so. But if I wake up and I'm like, "Hmmmm, I don't think I'm feeling that feminine today," then maybe I'll do a combination of like, you know, a cute shirt but then maybe some sweatpants, or something that looks a little more neutral—and then if I'm feeling more masculine then maybe I'll wear a flannel or something that tells everyone how I'm feeling.

It is important to note that not all people who are nonbinary experience their gender the same way Bird does—everyone is different. But for Bird, their gender fluctuates through the course of each day. Other nonbinary people may not identify with a gender at all, or their gender may fall somewhere in the middle of the gender spectrum. All of these genders are real and valid, and have existed for thousands of years in many different cultures! If someone says they are nonbinary, they are.

If you would like to explore the concepts of the gender spectrum or nonbinary genders further, there are many helpful resources out there, including, but certainly not limited to, the National Center for Transgender Equality's "Understanding Non-Binary People: How to Be

Respectful and Supportive" page[1] and the Trans Student Educational Resources webpage and "Gender Unicorn" tool.[2]

Cisgender

Cisgender (or cis), another adjective, is a term that refers to anyone who is not transgender. The Latin root "cis" is used in many settings, including geography and chemistry (Wu, 2015), and means "on the side of." Its first documented use in relation to gender was by sexologist Ernst Burchard in 1914 (Cava, 2016). Today, it is a widely accepted way to describe people whose gender exclusively aligns with their assigned sex at birth. For example, I am a cisgender woman because I identify as a woman and was assigned female at birth.

Some cisgender people reject this term, believing it to be a slur or to be unnecessary; however, "cis" is not a slur or a snub, and the term does not negate anyone's identity or gender. It is simply a descriptor, just as when discussing sexuality, "straight" is not an insult. And "cisgender" is easier to say than "non-transgender"!

Finally, cisgender refers to gender, not sexuality. Just as a person whose gender does not align with their assigned

---

1   https://transequality.org/issues/resources/understanding-non-binary-people-how-to-be-respectful-and-supportive

2   https://transstudent.org/gender

sex at birth can be gay, straight, queer, bisexual, asexual, etc., so can a cisgender person. Gender and sexuality are two different things.

Mirroring Language

You might be asking yourself, "Why are there only three terms defined in this chapter?" The answer is that language is always evolving, and even if I included an extensive glossary, it might be outdated by the time you read this!

Fortunately, terminology is not the end-all-be-all. Even if you have an encyclopedic knowledge of language about gender diversity, it doesn't necessarily result in you being a more effective ally. Furthermore, each individual may use different vocabulary to describe gender-related phenomena. For example, in my research, people used a variety of terms when discussing their deadnames (the names on original birth certificates that are no longer used): one alternated between using the terms "legal name" and "deadname," another consistently referred to his deadname as his "birth name," and a third participant called this his "given name."

If you are speaking with someone and they are using terms with which you are unfamiliar, it is a good practice to mirror language. Use of mirroring language is also a widely applied tool in counseling practice to facilitate conversations (Bryant-Jefferies, 2004; Deblinger *et al.*, 2015). So if someone, as above, talks about their deadname, it is appropriate to use that term with them during your conversation. If someone says "birth name" rather than "deadname," use the term they use. It's as simple as that.

By listening to people's own descriptions of what they are experiencing in terms of gender, those striving to ally with trans and nonbinary folks can support them by using their own terminology, rather than ascribing other language to them based on our own perceptions or knowledge.

If you would like to explore an extensive glossary of words related to LGBTQ+ folks and issues, I encourage you to visit the PFLAG website[3] (an organization that supports lesbian, gay, bisexual, transgender, and queer people, their parents and families, and allies), which is updated regularly.

Now that you understand some concepts and basic terms related to gender, let's talk about other types of language: specifically, the importance of using people's self-ascribed names and pronouns.

How We Refer to People: Names, Honorifics, and Pronouns

As I wrote at the beginning of this chapter, language is constantly evolving, and it is important to consider who is creating language, in particular language that excludes or limits. For example, whole populations have been

---

3   http://pflag.org/glossary

diminished through inadvertent and sometimes purposeful speech for hundreds of years, e.g., "All men are created equal," "One small step for man," etc. Language is now becoming more inclusive, and in terms of gender, many terms now exist that have been created by members of the LGBTQIA+ (lesbian, gay, bisexual, transgender, queer, intersex, and asexual/agender) community themselves to more accurately describe sexualities and genders that fall along the spectrum.

Using a person's name, honorific, and pronouns correctly, whatever they are, is important in affirming who that person is. The name I prefer people to use is "Christy," and I use she/her pronouns. It would be very confusing and uncomfortable if someone refused to use my name or pronouns correctly! This chapter discusses why using people's names and pronouns is essential. I also present approaches to learning and properly using people's names and pronouns.

Names

We are all given names at birth. Some of us like our names, some don't. Some of us use nicknames or our middle names, or change our names just because we want to. In all of these cases, we expect that others will use the names that we give them and ask them to use. For example, my brother's legal birth name was James, but when he was born everyone in the family called him "Jamie." When he decided in third grade that he preferred "James," his teachers and our family made the switch too. When he finally asked us to call him "Jay" in middle school, we changed how we addressed him again. It was simple for us to make these adjustments, and it made Jay more comfortable.

This may seem like a simple concept, but you would be surprised how many trans people are challenged by other people when they change their name. Here's the bottom line: names are important, and it is essential that we use the names that people wish us to use.

Often, it just takes a bit of practice to make this type of adjustment. If we have known someone by one name for a long time, it takes a bit of effort to remember to use a new name. The good news is that every one of us has done this many times in our lives when we call a bride who has adopted her husband's last name by her new last name. So this is very doable!

When I first came out as trans, I was like, "Hey, I don't use that name anymore. I use these pronouns." Some people I knew were great, but some of them were like, "Well, I'll try, but like, I'm going to mess up a lot. It's going to be kind of hard." And I understand, like I have a lot of friends who are trans, like my best friend is nonbinary and I've known them since they were like seven years old when they went by different pronouns and a different name. And they've changed their name four different times at this point. And it takes a little bit to get it, but you get it if you try.—Julian

As Julian highlights above, it just takes a bit of practice to remember to use a new name for someone. This may be as easy as visualizing someone's face and practicing saying their name several times. This is akin to learning new vocabulary when acquiring a new language. Practice in the shower, on walks, or on the commute to work to get used to a new term.

While most people make the effort to learn and use a new name, there are some who refuse to do so, and some even use a person's deadname as weaponized language to hurt someone. For example, Charles, a university student, shared the following story with me:

> *I had a teacher (in high school)—he made a comment that I will NEVER forget. I was saying something rude in class and he yelled back at me that I had an attitude problem. I was done listening to what he said and ignored him, and he called me by my full birth name. He called me by my birth name. As a punishment in front of my entire class. And my head SNAPPED around. And I was like—I started swearing at him, I went ballistic, I had absolutely no self-control, I had never been so angry in my life.*

In this case, the teacher decided to use Charles' deadname to get his attention and strike a blow. Not only was this action inappropriate, as the teacher knew he should be using Charles' name correctly, but his action also caused Charles to experience a raised level of anxiety such that he stopped attending class for several weeks and missed important instruction. Now consider how these dynamics may also occur in family, work, social, and community domains. How might this play out in another setting, and how can it be avoided?

As Sam Reidel, transgender author and columnist, writes:

> Hearing a blatantly masculine or feminine name applied to you when you're trying to realign your gender in a different direction can be a source of profound, dysphoria-inducing anxiety. Hearing or seeing one's old name can induce a visceral sense of terror that no matter how much progress one makes in their transition, the person they used to be (or pretended to be) is still there. (Reidel, 2017)

Conversely, using a trans person's name correctly sends a positive message of affirmation and support. Julian, who we heard from earlier, recounted the following story that illustrates the power of accepting and using a new name:

> *I was home for a visit and a mom of one of my cisgender friends approached me and she was like, "So Katherine has told me that I should call you Julian now. Is that right?" And I was like, "Yes." And she's like, "I'm so happy for you! I just love the shift so much!" And for the whole dinner she and her husband gendered me correctly and called me by the right name. At that time I was still getting misgendered all the time and was still being called my birth name a lot.*

So seeing adults that I didn't really know that well make that effort and be really excited for me made me so happy.

It takes little effort to call someone by their chosen name, but it can make a profound impact. It is really the least we can do to support and affirm trans people in our lives, in our communities, and in the media.

Using a transgender or nonbinary person's name correctly is not only an important practice to engage in when we are with them. It is also something that we need to do when the person is not present. For example, when in a group of cisgender people, if someone uses a deadname, it is appropriate to correct them ("Actually, he goes by Julian"). These types of reminders are not "calling out" one another, but rather, they are a way to support each other in efforts to support more inclusive communities.

Honorifics

Honorifics are titles that we use to show respect. They typically come before someone's name, such as "Ms." or "Mr." Honorifics are not only a way to indicate politeness, but they also tell us information about the person to whom they refer. For example, "Mrs." indicates a woman who is married, while "Miss" denotes an unmarried woman.

Many honorifics also tell us about gender: "Mr." is for men, "Miss," "Mrs.," or "Ms." are for women. But just as "Ms." is an honorific that was created to avoid defining a women's marital status in her title, there are also gender-neutral honorifics that do not indicate someone's gender. One example is "Mx." (generally pronounced "Mix"), a grammatically correct pronoun for people who do not exclusively identify as one gender. In the 2020 Gender Census worldwide online survey of 24,576 nonbinary people, 28% of respondents indicated that they use the honorific "Mx." (Gender Census, 2020).

Other widely used gender-neutral honorifics are associated with careers, such as "Dr." or "Rev."

Just as it is correct to use an individual's name in the way that they wish, true allies will take care to use a person's honorific appropriately and consistently.

Pronouns

Many of us are used to assigning pronouns to people without thinking about it, based on how we perceive someone's appearance and gender expression (gender expression is the way someone presents themselves to the world). For example, if a person appears female according to our society's unwritten rules, people typically use "she/her/hers" pronouns. Once again, this practice is rooted in our learned habits and unconscious biases. Being more thoughtful about pronouns and embracing the idea that we cannot assume someone's gender by looking at them is a practice that has the potential to create environments that support not only transgender and nonbinary people, but also cisgender people whose gender expression does not align with traditional ideas about what a woman or a man is "supposed" to look like.

Some cisgender people feel it is unnecessary to share their pronouns, that they are already implied. I have also had people say to me, "I don't use pronouns," but of course, they do! We all use personal pronouns, regardless of whether we are cisgender or transgender. My father's pronouns are he/him/his, so when someone describes something he did, they may say, "He went to the store."

When someone says, "I don't use pronouns," the underlying message is, "I don't have to think about my pronouns, and you should just assume my pronouns by looking at me." This perspective comes from a place of cisgender privilege (more on cisgender privilege later). Part of striving to be a true ally is recognizing that many trans people, as well as some cisgender people, are regularly misgendered when people use incorrect pronouns for them. This practice can lead to stress, anxiety, and frustration.

As Dr. Lee Airton writes on their webpage, *They is My Pronoun*:

Most people who have not had to ask others to use a particular pronoun do not realize how good it can feel when someone gets it right, or shows you they are trying. You can generate so much happiness, make such a large contribution to someone's well-being, and even make someone feel better about being in a workplace or group or get-together, just by using the pronoun they ask for…You can make someone want to come back to your office, clinic, store, house, or Facebook page. It is truly astonishing what a difference this can make. (2012)

In addition to making people feel welcome and validated in our spaces, using pronouns correctly also sends a message that we should not make assumptions about gender. This is why I recommend sharing our own pronouns whenever we can, even if people typically use our pronouns correctly based on how they perceive our gender. This can be done in a variety of ways:

- In a work meeting where everyone shares their name and role (for example, "I'm Sally, my pronouns are she/her, and I am a program manager").

- In a virtual call or conference where we can add our names and pronouns to our video (for example, "Sally Smith, She/Her").

- In an email signature (for example, "Sincerely, Sally Smith, Pronouns: She/Her").

The more we share our pronouns, the more we challenge the idea that we can assume someone's gender by looking at them. Doing this consistently also communicates that pronouns may change over time, so it's a good idea to share our pronouns more than once, even with the same group of people.

Fernando Zweifach López, Executive Director of San Diego LGBT Pride, shared an example of a time when correct usage of their pronouns was especially affirming on a special day for them:

The [representative from the county] told me, "You're getting your own day." So now I'm standing at the dais at the county office with the elected officials there. The room was full of community members and citizens that were there for different items that were being taken up that day for discussion. And as the supervisor read my name and read the proclamation, they used gender-neutral pronouns— my proper pronouns. And it just was this huge relief that someone on that person's staff made sure to get the right pronouns, made sure to coach him in advance and prepare him. And so here, in front of this whole room of folks, my proper pronouns are being used.

And because it was an elected official saying it out to the room, no one was talking back in this space where it was majority conservative folks, no one was making a weird comment or a face, and so I got to stand there and get this proclamation and be like, "Wow, this is really because of who I am holistically." I didn't have to receive this proclamation that had wrong pronouns. I wasn't introduced to a room full of people with the wrong pronouns. And it was such a huge moment and that allowed me to appreciate it fully.

Even on this day when Fernando was being honored by

the county, they went into the situation concerned that people would not remember to use their correct pronouns; the relief that Fernando felt when they realized that the elected official was using the proper pronoun allowed them to enjoy that moment. This is just one example of the power of pronouns and the importance of making sure each person's pronoun is used correctly.

All of this said, there are some points to consider: first, just because you share your pronoun does not mean that everyone else will automatically will feel comfortable doing so. Some people only share their pronouns in certain spaces. Instead, look at this practice as leading by example and sending a message in your spaces that gender diversity is acknowledged and accepted.

Also, if you are going to adopt the practice of sharing your pronouns, please do this consistently, and not only if you perceive there to be a trans person present. Sharing our pronouns in situations where we believe everyone in the room is cisgender is a way to gently push against systems that cause harm to trans people. It can also be a great way to open the door to conversations with people who may want to learn more! If another cisgender person asks you why you are sharing your pronoun, this is an opportunity to explain that we can't assume someone's gender because of how they look or sound.

Finally, if a person changes their pronoun, the correct approach is to use the new name and pronoun consistently when speaking about them, even when speaking about a time when they may have used a different name or pronoun. This is because while this information may be new for you, the trans person may have known for a long time that they were actually a different gender. For example, consider the following statements referring to someone who was assigned female at birth but now uses the name "Joseph" and "he/him" pronouns:

Incorrect: "When Joseph was little, she used to be afraid of thunderstorms."

Correct: "When Joseph was little, he used to be afraid of thunderstorms."

Statements like the incorrect one above can lead to confusion, or worse, could reveal information that someone is not comfortable with you sharing about them.

In conclusion: pronouns are important! Bird spoke with me about changing their pronoun on Facebook, and said, "It's not something you notice often but it means a lot to me—it's fantastic." Just as with learning a new name, it may take a bit of effort to use a different pronoun than the one we are used to, but practice makes perfect, and can be very helpful in reinforcing our use of correct pronouns.

Speaking fluent "they"

Not everyone uses he/him or she/her pronouns. As discussed earlier in the book, many people are nonbinary.

While nonbinary genders have been embedded in cultures across the world for centuries, this may still be a new idea for people who were taught that there are only two genders, and using pronouns other than he/his or she/hers can take some getting used to.

While pronouns like "he" and "she" are typically aligned to a specific gender, there are also pronouns that do not indicate a masculine or feminine gender. These are called gender-neutral pronouns. There are many types of gender-neutral pronouns, including Spivak or neo-pronouns, that have been used in English for many years, including ze/zir, sie/hir, and others.

"They" as a singular pronoun has also been widely accepted as a grammatically correct personal pronoun. Using singular "they" when referring to a person who uses that pronoun is specifically approved by the APA (American Psychological Association) and *The Chicago Manual of Style*. In 2019, singular "they" was even designated the "word of the year" by the Merriam-Webster Dictionary!

Unfortunately, some people refuse to exert the required effort to use singular "they" when appropriate. I have had people tell me, "I support trans people—of course I do—but I was an English major! You can't expect me to use 'they' to describe one person." However, using singular "they" as a pronoun for someone who uses it *is* correct grammar, so it is simply a matter of understanding and accepting that language evolves, as well as making the effort to get comfortable using people's pronouns.

As an aside, "they" is not the only pronoun whose use

has shifted over time; in fact, the word "you" was initially plural, which is why it always takes a plural verb even when referring to a single person (Merriam-Webster, 2019). Language can change, and we are living in an exciting time where language is becoming more inclusive and reflective of people's identities!

But what about making a pronoun switch for someone you have known for a long time? Again, this type of change takes effort but is so important in respecting and affirming the people in our families and communities. In explaining how this worked in her family when her first trans child shared their gender status and new pronoun "they" with the family, Maria told me:

> *We did some work ourselves around learning. My wife and I had been more familiar with the concept of a gender binary—most of the trans folks that we had encountered were transitioning within the binary, you know? The idea of being nonbinary was new to us, but we wanted to understand and learn, not just for our child Jackson, but also for any other folks we might come into contact with.*
>
> *Are we going to fumble? Yes. But we never questioned whether Jackson had a right or whatever you want to call it to be nonbinary and ask us to use these pronouns. To me, learning to speak "fluent they," to use "they" as a singular, which I know is so challenging, is so important. It's one of the things I think people don't understand about how affirming it is to use that pronoun for a child or an adult who feels that "they" more accurately reflects who they are.*

As a result of the work Maria's family did in actively learning about nonbinary identities and exerting efforts to become "fluent in 'they'" to support Jackson, Jackson understood that they were supported and loved for who they were.

If you would like to explore how to use gender-neutral/gender-inclusive pronouns, I highly recommend visiting the Minus 18 website and exploring their fun and informative "Pronouns" practice app that runs users through examples of how different pronouns are used in various cases.[4]

Finally, if you don't know what someone's pronoun is, it's okay to ask! I recommend doing this in a private conversation rather than in front of a group. It is also a good idea to share your pronoun first. You can simply say, "Hi, I'm Sally and I use she/her pronouns. How should I refer to you?/What pronouns should I use for you?" Notice that I'm not using the term "preferred" pronoun. The reason for this is that using the term "preferred" can imply that someone's pronouns are not valid. Just as a cis person has their pronouns (not "preferred" pronouns), so does a trans person.

Now that we have tackled the importance of using names and pronouns correctly, regardless of gender, let's consider how embedded gendered language is in our daily conversations and think about ways we might shift our use of language in more inclusive directions.

---

4   https://pronouns.minus18.org.au

Gendered Language

People often default to using language that they are used to, and a lot of the language we use emphasizes gender—even when it is not necessary or meaningful. Unfortunately, this can lead to some members of our communities being excluded. Thinking about our language habits and making efforts to speak in more inclusive ways is a big step in striving towards allyship.

In my role as an educator, I often hear teachers calling students to attention by saying, "Boys and girls," or grouping students by gender for lines or games. This is a problem for two reasons: first, it assumes incorrectly that all students fall into a gender binary; and more importantly, in my opinion, is that this practice can cause anxiety for students who may have questions about their gender and what that means. For example, law student Charles relayed the following memory from when he was in kindergarten that caused him significant stress:

I remember being very confused when people would separate things by gender, they would say, "Boys on one side and girls on the other," and I would freeze and everyone would laugh because they thought I was kidding, but I was genuinely confused as to where I was supposed to go because the person that I viewed myself as and the person that everybody else viewed me as was so different.

In fact, reminders about gender are all around us, and often, these are delivered in the form of language. But once we understand and acknowledge that gender does not exist within a binary, we can become conscious of how frequently gendered language is used, often unnecessarily.

For people who fall outside of the gender binary, this can be extremely frustrating, as their genders are not acknowledged; as Bird puts it:

> *People should stop saying the phrase "he or she"... People don't like using "they" as an ambiguous term for someone from any gender—I see ["he or she"] a lot and I'm like, "It's exclusionary! It's rude!"*

Phrases like "he or she," "boys and girls," and "ladies and gentlemen" also serve to reinforce the concept of the gender binary and reproduce structures and systems that cause harm to people who do not neatly fit into that system.

Often, simply becoming aware of the overuse of gendered language is enough to encourage people to consider alternatives. The following table presents some common phrases that incorporate unnecessary gendered language, and suggests more inclusive alternatives.

Try this, not that!

Instead of...	Try...
Welcome, ladies and gentlemen!/ Hi guys!	Welcome, everyone!/Welcome, all!/Welcome, friends!
What a beautiful baby boy/girl!	What a beautiful baby!
Is that your brother/sister?	Is that your sibling?
Each person entering must remove his/her shoes.	Guests must remove their shoes.

Gendered language also extends to niceties and manners. Depending on our cultural backgrounds and where we are from, many people are taught to address someone using "Ma'am" or "Sir." Of course, this practice is typically rooted in an assumption of someone's gender based on how they look or sound, which should be avoided. As Fernando recommends:

> You have to learn how to deconstruct those polite things that we were taught as children. And it's hard to unlearn that and adopt new practice in a way that feels comfortable for you. That still means that you can still be polite and have common courtesy and hold the door open for someone, but you don't have to refer to their gender and make assumptions.

Now that you understand how gendered language unnecessarily seeps into daily conversation to reinforce the status quo of a gender binary, the next step is considering the societal structures that reinforce norms and reproduce that status quo, as well as thinking about ways that we might evaluate and challenge these structures to make life better for all of us, regardless of gender.

The following chapter addresses the challenges inherent in societal expectations and assumptions related to gender for both cisgender and transgender people, and offers suggestions for reconsidering how we approach gender in our workplaces, families, and communities.

THINKING ABOUT GENDER

If you are cisgender and did not major in gender studies in school, chances are that you have not spent a lot of time thinking about gender; maybe for you, gender just "is;" something that exists on its own and happens in the background. However, gender is not such a simple concept and is tied to socialization, elements of biology, and our own understanding of who we are. This chapter is an introduction to thinking about gender on a deeper level and how gender impacts all of our lives.

Expectations and Performing Gender

Our society is the gender police and they want your gender identity or gender expression to align in a certain way— what they might consider normative. And frankly, to me, it's exhausting.—Maria

All of us, regardless of whether we are cisgender or transgender, participate in gender and have had experiences with expectations tied to gender. Earlier, I wrote about how gender is assigned to us at or before birth. We don't come into the world knowing what a "boy" or a "girl" is and what that means for us. Rather, gender is primarily socially constructed, and how gender is enacted varies depending on each society's expectations and norms. Scholar Judith Butler (who uses she/they pronouns) extensively explores the concept of gender performativity in her books, which I highly recommend. They write that gender is "instituted through a stylized repetition of acts" (Butler, 1988, p.519); we are taught how to perform our gender by family, peers, and media from the moment we are born.

When I reflect on my own childhood, I consider that I was surrounded by lessons about how to perform femininity; from playing with Barbies to being dressed in frilly skirts to watching my mother put on makeup and heels before going out, I understood at a very early age what expectations and norms were in regard to how to behave, dress, and act. My brother learned that he had a very different set of expectations associated with gender; his peers regularly policed his behavior and affect in elementary school, making fun of him when he showed emotion or did not perform masculinity like a "tough guy."

When one begins examining society through the lens of gender expectations and how they serve to reproduce societal norms and structures, it's almost like taking the red pill and seeing the unpleasant truth of "The Matrix" for the first time (as an aside, sisters Lana Wachowski and Lilly Wachowski who directed that movie are both trans!). From clothing options to television shows to advertisements and everything in between, we are reminded throughout the course of each day how we are expected to behave, look, sound, and interact within strict, unwritten gender rules. These rules are not universal, and vary by culture. Case in point, the following is a true story that happened to me in Japan in 2003.

After spending a long day in the recording studio singing songs with my jazz vocal group, my Japanese bandmate and I stepped outside onto the frenetic streets of Tokyo in search of food. We entered a convenience store lit up with neon lights and festooned with advertising signs.

The cashier, a man in his forties, immediately bellowed a loud, "Irasshaimase!," which is a traditional commercial greeting in Japan that translates to, "Welcome to the store!" We nodded, smiled, and began our search for sustenance.

I spoke very little and read no Japanese, so my strategy was to analyze the artwork on the packages to determine their contents. I found a bag of rice snacks, which I considered a safe purchase; however, when I approached the cashier and placed the bag on the counter, he furrowed his eyebrows and shook his head, a bemused smile on his face.

I immediately felt self-conscious. Had I done

something wrong? Was I not supposed to place the bag on the counter?

My friend joined me and he and the cashier whispered for a moment, after which point he laughed and said, "Those are men's snacks."

"What are you talking about?" I answered, completely taken aback.

He was clearly getting a kick out of my faux pas as he quietly laughed, "Those are for men to drink with beer."

I could feel my face getting red. Although I was embarrassed at my mistake, the whole idea of "snacks for men" was baffling to me.

I decided to "rebel" and purchase the rice crisps anyway, and scooted out of the store as quickly as possible, to the amusement of my bandmate and the cashier. Happily, no snack police showed up to arrest me, and the rice cakes tasted good, even if I was a woman!

Why am I sharing this story? Because this is just one, miniscule example of how expectations and norms involved with gendered systems are ridiculous, and how they shift in different cultures. I was on the other side of the globe and was not familiar with the gender norms there that dictated that my choice was inappropriate...but c'mon, just give me a snack!

Part of being a true ally is to avoid reinforcing power structures that replicate cisnormativity (the idea that cisgender boys/girls are the "correct" default). But if we don't actively think about what we do on a daily basis and instead rely on habit, it is easier than one may think to engage in rituals that normalize and reinforce cisnormativity.

For example, note the phenomenon of the "gender-reveal party" in which expecting parents reveal to family and friends the assigned sex of their yet unborn baby, often by cutting into a cake to reveal a pink or blue interior to indicate if the baby is a "girl" or a "boy." While so many of us take every opportunity to celebrate aspects of birth and childhood, we must ask ourselves: is this new and evolving tradition having its own unintended consequences? Clearly, the underlying assumption of a gender-reveal party is that the baby will be cisgender, which we honestly do not know when the baby is in utero. "Is it a boy or a girl?" basically translates to, "Does the baby have a penis or a vulva?"

In cases like this, assigning gender is deeply linked to the story that we tell ourselves about what the baby will do, look like, act like. Once we have assigned this label of "boy" or "girl" we are unconsciously reinforcing a gender binary and placing a heavy burden on the child to behave and look in the way we expect.

In every society, gender norms and expectations are different, and if you don't know the rules and abide by them unquestioningly, you can't succeed at playing the game of gender. But in this game, there are few winners. The game upholds patriarchy and is rigged for those at the center of the wheel of power to be the winners. Those who are not at the center experience increased levels of marginalization and oppression.

The trauma caused by these unwritten gender rules is illustrated by the extremely high numbers of trans people who face physical violence. As I mentioned earlier, 2020 saw the highest number of violent deaths for trans people, the majority of whom were Black and Latinx transgender women (Human Rights Campaign, 2020). In addition, a recent survey by The Trevor Project indicates that more than half of transgender and nonbinary youth have considered suicide (The Trevor Project, 2019). Clearly, work needs to be done to dismantle the societal structures that hurt those who are not interested in or able to follow the rules of the gender game.

To do this, we each need to acknowledge our own privilege and consider ways to make space for those who do not benefit in the same way from the intersecting elements of their identities. Privilege in this case does not mean that we do not experience challenges or strife; of course, we all encounter difficulties. Rather, it acknowledges that some of us do not face the same obstacles that others do because of who we are. The next section addresses the concept of cisgender privilege and how we must consider issues of cis privilege when striving towards allyship.

Is Cisgender Privilege a "Thing?"

Short answer: much of the time, cisgender people experience privilege based on their gender status. Most often, as a cisgender man or woman, you will not be challenged when entering a washroom or purchasing clothing that aligns with your perceived gender. You will not be challenged when you talk about your gender or be told your gender is "fake." People will use your name and pronouns without questioning them.[1]

Some cisgender people have even expressed discomfit at use of the term "cisgender;" this is on par with some cis people claiming they, "don't have a pronoun," and comes from a point of privilege. As Karen Pollock writes in their essay "Cis is Not a Slur": "In saying we both wear labels, have identities, we are challenging the idea there is a default and an other, and that the default is only known as normal" (Pollock, 2018). In other words, by saying we don't need a label for cisgender people, it assumes that cisgender is the "correct" way to be. Years ago, some people made the same argument that while "gay" and "lesbian" were necessary terms, "straight" was not, and people should not be labeled "straight." Just as "white" is a descriptor for race and "straight" is a descriptor for sexuality, "cisgender" is simply a way to differentiate and describe someone who is not trans, and is not a derogatory term.

---

[1] Want to learn more about cisgender privilege? Sam Killermann presents a more extensive list of ways cisgender people benefit from privilege on the website, http://itspronouncedmetrosexual.com.

"Tomboys" and "Sissies"

Cis privilege occurs because of the perception that someone is aligned with their assigned sex at birth; however, it is also possible to be cisgender but be persecuted because of being gender non-conforming (not looking, sounding, or acting according to societal norms related to one's gender). For example, in his book *Beyond Trans: Does Gender Matter?* Heath Fogg Davis writes, "As a 'tomboy' who preferred and was allowed by my parents to wear boy's clothing, and keep a short haircut, I was routinely questioned and reprimanded by girls and women for being in the 'wrong' public bathroom" (2017, pp.7–8).

This gets back to the idea of performing gender, and how gender-based expectations can lead to strife. Those whose gender expression, behavior, and physical attributes align with the restricted concepts of how others believe people should look and act have an easier time navigating through the world. Those who don't often experience marginalization and trauma. We have all seen boys who act "too feminine" being called "sissies" or other derogatory names when others disapprove of their expression or behavior, or girls being called "tomboys" because they enjoy sports or do not present in a traditionally "feminine" way. These are examples of how expectations about gender and the privilege inherent in "passing" as cisgender are important to acknowledge if we are to address changes that should be made in our families, schools, and communities.

As a white, cisgender woman who is perceived by

others to be such, I recognize that I benefit from layers of privilege, and understand that I have a responsibility to constantly unpack my own bias, expand my knowledge, and actively engage in practices that will create a more inclusive community for people of all genders. This leads me to the next chapter of the book, which dives into what it means to engage in allyship work with trans and nonbinary individuals and communities.

HOW CAN I STRIVE TO
BE A TRUE ALLY?

This chapter presents a story of allyship, told in the words of Julian, who was assigned female at birth, and Shawna, who are members of the same community vocal ensemble (The Melodies). The Melodies was an all-female group at the time that Julian auditioned and was accepted. Over the course of their time in the group, Julian's understanding of his gender shifted, and rather than this causing strife, the ensemble evolved along with Julian.

As you read the story, consider the ways that this ensemble strove to ally with Julian as he disclosed information about his gender, and reflect upon how this ultimately benefited all members of the group.

A Story of True Allyship

Julian: When I auditioned for The Melodies, I was still identifying as gender-fluid, but I wasn't out to everybody, and I wasn't super vocal about what pronouns I wanted. Most people assumed I was just female, and people who did know that I wasn't identifying as just female were still using she/her pronouns. So when I auditioned, I didn't feel like I had to be in a co-ed ensemble. I was just like, "Either is fine."

Shawna: Singing in general is polarized when it comes to gender, you know, between dress code and voice parts. Soprano and alto are women, and tenors and basses are men. And so when we first had this all-female group, we were like, "This is our identifying factor. We're going to go to all these competitions and sing about female empowerment and you know, that's going to be our message." And it really wasn't until Julian brought it up, that we were like, "Wait—this could be different!"

Julian: So at some point after I joined the group, I mentioned in a rehearsal that actually, I was not a girl, that I was nonbinary.

Shawna: My first reaction was, I don't know what this means for the group, but I know that he's an important part of the group. And I know that whatever we decide, he needs to feel comfortable because I want to keep him in the group, and I'm sure everybody else feels the same way.

So some of the people who maybe just weren't as familiar with LGBT folks, they were kind of like, "How does this fit into a musical context? Because this is our group's identity and we don't want to change that." And Julian was very patient and when people would kind of voice their concerns respectfully, he would say, "I understand that that's been the message before, but I love being in the group and I still want to be here. I just want to make sure that we're not brushing my gender aside because that's an important part of me."

Julian: Everyone was really accepting and really great. We just kind of went on from there, but then at the start of the following year, I realized that the label "trans" actually described me better, and I wanted to use he/him pronouns. And that led to us having to have some conversations in the group because it's a big step from, "Oh, I identify as something that's more nonbinary" to, "I'm a boy, actually!" And so we can't really call ourselves an all-female ensemble.

Shawna: When Julian first disclosed to us that he was trans, there were a couple of members who were like, "But I still want to sing about female empowerment and I still want that to be our group's identity." And so there were a lot of really difficult discussions around what mattered more to us: having every member in the group feel valid, or having a message of female empowerment.

Julian: At first it was a little bit difficult. There was a little bit of tension because we realized we needed to change the branding of the group. Calling it an all-female group at that point was incorrect. But some people who I think are a little bit more ignorant of that sort of stuff were like, "Girl power has always been so important to our vibe. It defines us as a group. And I just don't know if I want to change." But that didn't last very long because very quickly, the Music Director decided that we should all have a meeting to talk about how we want to brand the group going forward and what this means.

She privately messaged me before making that statement and asked if I wanted to speak about what I wanted and how I felt. She told me, "I don't want to put you on the spot, but if this is something that you want to talk about, I want you to feel like we're hearing you." And I said, "Definitely, I want to talk about this!" The Music Director set the tone of the discussion and made it clear that the question was not, "DO we change branding?" but "HOW do we change?" That discussion was actually really good.

Shawna: Julian is absolutely fantastic. One of the things we talked about was our repertoire, because one of the songs in our repertoire was "Natural Woman." And so he said, "I'm still comfortable singing the song because I'm also all about female empowerment, even though I don't identify as female." And so that really swayed the people who were unsure that it was okay to brand ourselves as a "treble voice" group and take the emphasis off the gender and focus it more on our sound.

Julian: Even the people who had been a little bit resistant, once I explained why it was so important to me and what it meant, really understood and were completely on board. I think the initial resistance by a few was motivated by not fully understanding what acknowledging my gender in the group meant to me and how important it was. And very quickly everyone was completely on board and really accepted the idea of moving from the idea that, "We're an all-female group" to "We're a treble (voice) group."

Shawna: Through this process, I think we really educated each other. We tried to avoid putting pressure on Julian because he was already going through so much coming out to us, coming out to his family, his friends—that's a lot to deal with. So if we had questions, we could go to the Music Director, we could go to each other.

Julian: The Music Director handled it extremely well, on two major different fronts. First, she set the expectation that some change was required and she started the conversation. And she also really centered me in the conversation by asking me if I wanted to share how I was feeling and what I wanted. Not that I'm the only one who makes a decision, but it's really important for me to have a say, which is super important, like feeling that my voice is valued and really heard.

Pretty quickly, the members of The Melodies became some of my biggest champions. When I came out a lot of the members hyped me up and remembered to gender me correctly. It was just very supportive and whenever someone messed up my pronouns, they pretty much always corrected themselves quickly. And they were some of the first people to consistently use my correct name. So they were really a massive support system.

Shawna: I was definitely guilty of making mistakes a couple of times. I don't think there was a member in the group who always got it perfect. But we were there to help each other because we knew we wanted Julian to be comfortable. So even if we were having a discussion, if we were in a sectional and he wasn't there and someone said something about Julian and accidentally misgendered him, then you know, another person would speak up and say, "Oh, don't forget. Julian uses he/him pronouns." So it was very comfortable once we crossed that border. I think that's a really important component of allyship: being vocal when your friend isn't there, you know what I mean? So holding each other accountable, regardless of whether or not your trans friend is around.

Julian: The members would also stick up for me when the group would be announced as an all-female group at competitions. They would say, "Hey, you can't do that."

It's so nice because it's hard as a trans person to always correct people. It gets really tiring, and sometimes people will get mad at you when you correct them, which can be a little scary. Having your friends join in with you when that happens can be really helpful.

Shawna: We never pushed it, but we didn't hesitate to correct people. I remember there was one specific example where we were working with someone from a professional all-female group, and the leader kept talking about how being in an all-female acapella ensemble is so great (assuming that we were all female). And then one of the quieter members of The Melodies who had never been very vocal in the discussions before raised her hand and she said, "Actually we identify as an all treble group because not everyone in the group identifies as female." So that was a really beautiful moment. And it was really just little things like that.

Julian: I felt like there was a concerted effort to validate my gender and who I was and also just celebrate it. Being able to talk with everybody as a group discussion really brought us together. It made us feel a lot closer and a lot more united—and that's not just my opinion, that's something some of the other members have said, that the journey we went through with all of this actually brought us a lot closer together. It made me feel like my voice and my needs are really centered and that I was being heard. And there's an atmosphere of support and inclusivity.

★ ★ ★

I love this story because it demonstrates how an entire community can benefit from allyship action. The musical group continues to thrive and successfully compete, and the members talk about how they feel a much stronger connection with one another as a result of learning about gender diversity and finding ways to listen to and support Julian. The following section breaks down the different elements of allyship in this story and talks about how these can be applied more generally to create gender-friendly spaces.

The Basics: Acknowledge and Listen

Most of my experiences have to do with allies not engaging in allyship and believing that simply not being actively transphobic is the allyship, but allyship is an active practice.—Chris

As Chris says in the quote above, allyship is active. One cannot be a true ally by sitting on the sidelines and being polite. The first step in this work is to acknowledge gender diversity and to listen to trans voices to build an understanding of what work is needed.

Acknowledge to Prevent "Gender-Evasiveness"

Reminders about gender are all around us. Whether we are walking through a department store with "men's" and "ladies'" sections, using sex-separated facilities such as locker rooms and restrooms, or watching television and seeing images of gender norms represented on the screen, we are being reminded about gender. However, many people are uncomfortable talking about or even acknowledging topics related to gender diversity.

I encounter this discomfort with acknowledging gender diversity in educational settings regularly. In one meeting on this topic, it quickly became clear through comments by the group members that most felt some anxiety about the correct approaches to supporting trans students. As a result, several educators avoided the topic completely in their teaching practice. One teacher shared her opinion on this lack of acknowledgement of gender diversity, saying:

> In the end [someone's gender] doesn't matter. What's important is the work they're doing, not how they identify. Which is the approach that I've had with my students... I kind of approach it as well—does it matter? I'm wrestling with the fact that if I treat you as a human being in my classroom and treat you fairly and don't even distinguish between a female, a male, a...binary? I'll be honest. To me the importance of the pronoun, it's hard for me—dealing with that. (quoted in Whittlesey, 2019)

This teacher, like all of us, wants to believe she is doing her best to be a good person, and truly thinks that she is treating everyone fairly by not acknowledging gender diversity. What she does not yet understand is that by ignoring gender altogether, she is failing to appreciate the different experiences and perspectives that people of varying genders can contribute to her classes.

Ignoring gender diversity is a troubling framework and parallels a "colorblind" ideology wherein white people claim not to "see" race or that race does not matter (Tarca, 2005). This phenomenon is more aptly described as "color-evasiveness" (Annamma, Jackson, & Morrison, 2017), as it involves purposefully ignoring the experiences of people of color. While some white people believe this is a helpful approach, it is actually harmful, as we can't address or improve something we can't or won't acknowledge. Color-evasiveness reinforces the status quo, doesn't allow us to appreciate individual differences, and prevents us from confronting and addressing our own personal biases (Kraehe & Brown, 2011; Leonardo & Porter, 2010; Thein, 2013).

Similarly, when cisgender people adopt a "gender-evasive" perspective and willfully ignore gender diversity, it reinforces systems that cause harm to transgender and nonbinary members of our communities, and sends the message that someone's gender is not acceptable to talk about (Bolger, 2016).

In the story of allyship in this chapter, there are several examples that illustrate how the members of the vocal group acknowledged Julian's gender status. As he says, "I felt like there was a concerted effort to validate my gender and who I was and also just celebrate it." Julian asserted that the group discussion made his voice feel heard, and the use of his newer names showed him that others supported him in his journey.

The way members of the group acted toward Julian had a positive effect:

People made an effort to gender me correctly. And to be really supportive and hype me up, which made me feel more like I have a right to be treated correctly. They were always hyping me up and were like, "Oh my gosh, King, you look so good!"

Gestures that emphasize acceptance and inclusion can be referred to as a "microaffirmations" (Flanders, 2015), defined as, "small, interpersonal interactions that communicate validation for an identity" (Pulice-Farrow, Bravo, & Galupo, 2019, p.45). Unlike microaggressions, which are subtle actions or statements that are discriminatory in nature and cause harm to marginalized individuals (Chang & Chung, 2015; Pulice-Farrow, Clements, & Galupo, 2017), repeated microaffirmations, such as consistently using a person's name and pronouns correctly or complimenting someone's appearance in a gender-affirming way, can result in a person feeling that their authentic gender is seen, affirmed, and celebrated (Anzani, Morris, & Galupo, 2019; Koch *et al.*, 2020).

One component of practicing microaffirmations is active listening (Powell, Demetriou, & Fisher, 2013), which involves focusing on clearly understanding what is being shared. We all need to be listened to, but sometimes rather than exerting the effort to understand what a transgender or nonbinary family member, friend, or colleague is really saying or asking for, cisgender people make assumptions. The next section addresses the importance of listening to trans and nonbinary individuals in order to be better allies, create equitable spaces, and protect their safety.

Listen

Listening allows us to center the needs of our trans and nonbinary community members. In the story of allyship above, Julian discusses how the Music Director made the point of centering Julian's voice in the conversation between ensemble members and how this made him feel that he was valued and heard:

> *An ally needs to center trans voices. A cis person doesn't know what trans people need because they're not trans. So you need to center the trans person themselves to hear what they specifically need. Like, "how can we best help you?", and then go from there.*

But I don't know any trans people...how can I listen?

If you are a cisgender person reading this book but you do not know anyone who is out as transgender or nonbinary (which doesn't actually mean you don't know any trans people, by the way!), you can still listen and learn from trans and gender-expansive individuals in a variety of ways. There are so many amazing resources available, including TransLash,[1] which presents stories of numerous trans folks in their own words to, "shift the cultural understanding of what it means to be transgender in order to foster social inclusion and reduce anti-trans hostility" (TransLash, n.d.).

In addition, the podcasts listed in the Resources section—some of my favorites—will provide you with access to a variety of trans voices. These are great resources for learning about different trans experiences.

Protecting Confidentiality

If a person shares their transgender or nonbinary status with you, that is a message of trust. Too often, gender-expansive individuals are faced with transphobia, disapproval, or in worst cases, violence in a variety of settings. This is why it is extremely important for cisgender people striving to be true allies to make sure to listen to trans and nonbinary friends to gauge in which settings the

---

1   http://translash.org

person feels safe "being out" with their authentic gender. As Chris explains it:

> *As far as ineffective engagements go, the biggest one is not checking in and trying to be an ally in a space that isn't safe. It's important to let the person you're attempting to be an ally for determine the method and if/when allyship is needed—especially for LGBTQIA2+ [lesbian, gay, bisexual, transgender, queer/questioning, intersex, agender/asexual and two-spirit] people, as you can "out" someone by trying to be an ally in a space where they haven't "come out."*

So, how does this look in practice?

As an educator working with trans and nonbinary students, I check in with them to learn from each person where and when it is safe for me to use their name and pronoun. If they prefer me to avoid using a particular name or pronoun in class discussions or even in conversations with their parents, it is my responsibility to honor this request and shift my approach (in the state where I work, protecting student confidentiality in these cases is actually required by law to protect student safety in situations where they may be in physical danger or experience a loss of housing status, i.e., be forced to leave the house by their families, if the family learns that they are transgender). There are Gender Support Plans available to support this process in school settings, and to make sure students' authentic genders will be acknowledged and affirmed in safe ways that give each student control over this process.[2] While this is a more structured approach to protecting confidentiality within schools, there are general approaches you can take wherever you are to make sure you are supporting your trans and nonbinary friends and colleagues in ways that also ensure they are safe.

In the story of allyship from this chapter, Julian discusses how the Music Director privately messaged him before facilitating a group discussion. The director said, "I don't want to put you on the spot, but if this is something that you want to talk about, I want you to feel like we're hearing you." At that point, Julian had already shared information about his gender with the ensemble, but the director's tact and thoughtful consideration of Julian's feelings was something that Julian appreciated.

Check-ins are important to ensure that cis individuals are not making assumptions about when and where a trans or nonbinary person might feel comfortable sharing their gender status. For example, Chris shared the following story with me about how allyship can look different in various settings:

The best allies are the ones that take the onus off of you to affirm yourself (after checking for permission). For instance, if you're in a place and getting misgendered, it can become stressful to constantly correct other people and when it happens enough in that space, you sometimes just want to leave the space and not return. I was part of a roller derby

---

2   https://genderspectrum.org/articles/using-the-gsp

league where I continuously got misgendered and felt like I corrected people maybe 20 times a practice, and let more instances of misgendering go. I had a teammate who would correct for me when she was at practice. So, one time, I was the jammer, and people were shouting, "She's coming, she's coming, she's here!" to communicate on the track and [my teammate] cut in, "They're coming," louder to correct it and addressed the members of the team after the jam ended about why she did that. I really appreciated that allyship. The same ally checked in with me at a different location where I wasn't "out" to see if she should also do that in the other environment and I told her not to because I wasn't sure about my safety in that space. So, it's always important to realize that what will affirm your friend in one space may also put them in danger in another and it's important to check in.

In general, if someone comes out to you as trans or nonbinary in a private setting, it is a good idea to ask in what spaces they may be comfortable with you using their authentic name and pronouns. Do they want to be "out" at work? With your friend group? In public? It is important to be cognizant of these circumstances when referring to your friend, whether or not they are present. Using a different name or pronoun in certain situations based on your friend's request to ensure their safety and confidentiality is a key component of allyship.

Asking questions is essential to ensure we are appropriately supporting our trans and nonbinary friends and colleagues, but consider that not all questions are appropriate to ask.

Asking Questions

It is always good to acknowledge gender diversity and it is important to ask questions when someone shares their gender status with you about how they want to be addressed in various situations. When wondering if other questions are appropriate to ask, it is important to consider the nature and depth of the relationship. A good rule of thumb is to ask yourself, "Would I ask this question of a cisgender person?" If the answer is no, skip it!

For example, imagine two work colleagues, Betty and Sue, are having a conversation after Sue has returned from a maternity leave:

Betty: Congratulations on the new baby!

Sue: Thank you, we are so happy he's healthy and doing well.

Betty: This is your third child, right?

Sue: That's right! The oldest is in kindergarten now.

Betty: That's a big family. Are you thinking about having your tubes tied now? I've heard a lot of women do that after they have three kids.

Sue: Um…that's a bit inappropriate to ask, isn't it???

While this scenario is not equivalent to a conversation between a cisgender person asking inappropriate questions of a transgender colleague, it does highlight how questions about another person's body or medical procedures are just not okay to ask.

Unfortunately, trans and nonbinary people are often asked inappropriate and unnecessary questions. Julian sums this up in the following statement:

> *I think some people might feel like they're walking on eggshells if they're like, "This is the first trans person I've met. What do I ask, can I ask questions?" In general if they share their gender status with you or whatever, the answer is, yeah, of course, we all have conversations about who we are as long as these questions are what you would ask any other person. You need to treat the trans person like you would anyone else, like they have basic dignity. Treat them with respect. Don't ask them questions that you wouldn't ask a cis person.*

Just as it is not okay to ask a cisgender person about their body history, whether they have had surgeries, or even about their genitalia, it goes without saying that it is unacceptable to ask a trans or nonbinary person these questions.

If you are reading this and realizing you have made mistakes like this, the good news is that you are taking steps to more appropriately support the trans people in your life. We need to decenter ourselves and realize that being an ally is not about looking or feeling good ourselves, but rather putting in the work to create more safe, equitable, and inclusive communities for us all.

Understand It's Not About You

Being an ally means you need to understand where a trans person is comfortable and where they're not and how you can make them most comfortable because their journey is not about you. It's about them. I think it's really recognizing that you're not the center of that story and you just need to do whatever they feel best with you doing.—Shawna

Being a true ally with the trans and nonbinary people in our lives and beyond involves effort. It is up to us to educate ourselves, use language appropriately, be mindful of the wishes of the trans people in our lives, and work to create more inclusive communities. But the effort required to do this pales in comparison to the effort that most trans and nonbinary people need to exert on a daily basis simply to be heard, affirmed, and safe.

Unfortunately, sometimes when a trans person asks a cis person to use a new name or pronoun, the cis person will respond by complaining about the effort this may require. Taking care to name and gender someone correctly is really the least we can do, and, as discussed earlier in the book, this is essential to affirm people's authentic genders.

Julian discussed this issue with me, describing an instance when a cisgender person told him:

> *"Well I'm going to try, but it's going to be really hard. And like, I'm probably going to forget a bunch, but okay. I'll do what I can." And that makes me feel like it's my fault for needing different pronouns and a different name and I'm asking too much when really she should have said, "Oh my gosh, all right. Yes, I will do that. That's great." I think cis people need to realize that that kind of a response really doesn't help or support the trans person; it just makes the trans person feel like they're being a burden and trans people are already unlikely to be super supported by those around them.*

In this conversation, the cis person centers herself. Rather than simply acknowledging Julian's request that she use a new name and pronoun for him, she instead communicated a message through her response that she was inconvenienced by the request. Sometimes this type of response comes from a place of defensiveness, as people might be nervous about making mistakes and are attempting to excuse potential misgendering because, "It's hard to remember." Decentering ourselves in these contexts and understanding that learning is a lifelong process can help to avoid falling into the defensiveness trap.

The idea of someone else's gender identity being

something that we cannot police or control is often a more significant issue for parents of trans or nonbinary youth, primarily because there are so many expectations embedded within the cisnormative society we live in. If a child is transgender, some parents may struggle with the discrepancy between their ideas about the child's gender and the child's authentic gender. For example, I once had conversations with a trans youth's parents who were coming to terms with the change in their child's gender status in different ways. While the mother was understanding and supportive, the father struggled to accept that the child was trans because he couldn't overcome the idea that his "little boy," who had now shared that she was a girl, would not grow up to "be like his dad." Over time, the father did become much more accepting of the child's gender status, but for some stressful months, his reluctance to initially accept his child as she was caused significant conflict within the family.

If a family member, including a child, shares that they are transgender or nonbinary, the best approach is to support them and center their experience and needs. I spoke with Maria, a parent of four children, two of whom are transgender, about her experience supporting her children through this process:

I think one of the things about our family's journey, that's maybe a little bit unique is that we have two children of our four children who identify as trans and their stories are very different. And some of that I think has to do with who they are as people, their personalities, their different experiences, and also they're about eight years apart in age.

So first I'll talk about our older child who is now 21 and at the age of 18 showed my wife a picture of a haircut they wanted to get. The haircut was quite different from the hair that they've had their whole life—long hair down the back, right to the top of the bum. To us, their long hair honestly always seemed a little out of place for the rest of our child's gender expression. There were times in Jackson's life when we questioned as parents what was going on with Jackson: is Jackson a sporty girl, is Jackson lesbian? We asked ourselves a lot of these questions because from a very young age, in terms of Jackson's gender expression, they dressed in a very neutral way.

So back to the beginning of the story where Jackson shows my wife this picture of a haircut that they want to get, and the haircut is very short, kind of buzzed around the sides. Then Jackson gets their hair cut. It's a drastic change, but really little else about them changes at that time. But a couple months later, Jackson sends us a Facebook message. Now, we see ourselves as very open and accepting parents. When we received the Facebook message, we were like, "Why can't Jackson just tell us face to face?" But this was Jackson's way to tell us because it was easier for them. And we got over that part very quickly because in a way it doesn't matter. What matters is your child is telling you, not which way they decide to do it, which I think is something that's helpful for people to know. It's a very challenging thing to talk about. And then to try to say everything you want to say face to face, it's hard. So the Facebook message came to both of us. It said, "I want you to know that basically I have been looking for words to describe myself, and this is my best sort of approximation after thinking about it for years." And they said, "I am nonbinary trans masculine."

And when we did some research into what that meant, everything sort of came together for us. We wanted to know how to best support Jackson, which for them was waiting for them to talk about things, not asking them questions. So we basically said, "We're here, if there's anything we can do or not do." And the idea of being nonbinary was new to us, so we did some work learning about it, not just for Jackson, but also for any other folks we might come into contact with in the future.

For our younger child, Bennie, the story was very different. In the spring of eighth grade year, we got a text saying, "I'm coming out as lesbian." At the time there were also some tumultuous things happening with Bennie around mental health issues, anxiety, depression, and self-harm, and we had a lot of concerns about his mental health. And so here we have this child who was assigned female at birth, who first comes out as lesbian. And then we get a text saying, "I'm transgender, I want [the first name that Bennie chose], and I want you to use he, him, and his pronouns." Okay. Then some weeks go by and all the while we're trying to find a therapist because there were clearly a lot of issues going on. Over time, Bennie told us he was nonbinary and we went with that, but ultimately he circled back to he, him and his pronouns and his current name. And I will say that since for the better part of a year now, Bennie is much happier. He more easily smiles, he feels more understood, I think. And there have been a few things that I feel have made a difference. One is us sort of giving our support no matter where he was on the journey. Because for him, it wasn't this linear thing, it was more of an exploration and we were like, "Wherever this goes, it goes."

Maria's transgender children had experiences that were considerably different, and this further amplifies the notion that there is no one trans experience. What *was* consistent in the stories is that Maria and her wife were supportive and understanding as their children shared their gender status with them, and that they educated themselves to adequately meet the needs of each child. As a result, both Jackson and Bennie are now thriving.

It probably comes as no surprise that a supportive home life can act as a buffer against negative health outcomes, including depression, for youth addressing gender identity questions and challenges (Ryan *et al.*, 2010). Some families respond to youth gender questioning in a positive manner; unfortunately, many do not, and often, families will completely reject youth who are not cisgender (Needham & Austin, 2010).

While family plays a vital role in transgender and non-binary youths' wellness, almost half of LGBTQ youth who are out to their families say that their families "make them feel bad for being LGBTQ;" of this group, trans youth are over twice as likely to be taunted or mocked by family for their gender identity than lesbian, gay, or bisexual youth whose gender identity corresponds with their assigned gender at birth (Kahn *et al.*, 2018).

For these reasons, transgender and nonbinary youth are at a higher risk than cisgender lesbian, gay, or bisexual youth for developing issues with drugs, risky sexual behavior, and self-harming or suicide (Nealy, 2017; The Trevor Project, 2019). Concurrently, young adults with high levels of family acceptance also experience higher self-esteem, social support, and general health as compared to youth whose parents are not accepting of their transgender identity and expression (Ryan *et al.*, 2010).

Considering these risks alone, it is clear that families must make efforts to educate themselves and provide a supportive home for their children, regardless of gender. Here, Maria explains the importance of decentering ourselves:

As parents, you sort of have to get out of your own way and think to yourself, "This is really not about me." And people will try to make it about you. I think we have the most trouble as cis people when our children go against whatever we've been taught are the norms, and worry about "What are people going to think? And what are people going to say?" But I think if your children know that you have an open mind and an open ear, and that you're going to be there for them, then they will risk telling you much more than if they don't know that those things are true. And there's sort of an old paradigm of, "The parents are the teachers and the children are the learners—I teach, you learn. I say what to do, and then you do it." But I think that our kids know that they can teach us too, you know? We're not in the business of deciding for children who they're going to be.

If you would like to learn more about supporting children who are transgender, nonbinary, or who may have questions about their gender, please explore the Human Rights Campaign's "Transgender Children & Youth: Understanding the Basics" page on their website.[3]

So far in this chapter, we have learned about the importance of decentering ourselves to be more effective allies for transgender and nonbinary folks. Part of this decentering involves being open when criticized or corrected rather than making things "about us." The following section delves into other ways that we can make sure we are truly centering our trans or nonbinary community members in our interactions.

Defensiveness

Before we know it, we can't know it. But once we know it, then it's our job to do better.—Maria

---

3   www.hrc.org/resources/transgender-children-and-youth-understanding-the-basics

A couple of years ago, I led a workshop for graduate students at a local university who were studying education. During one of our discussions, a man in his mid-twenties began sharing about a recent encounter in a class he had been teaching: "I called this student's name, and she got all upset, telling me to call her by another name. She called me out in front of the whole class. So what was I supposed to do?" It was clear from his tone of voice that this situation had made him feel uncomfortable and embarrassed, and he was angry at the student for correcting him publicly. This type of situation happens all the time, and it is up to us to decide how we react. We can either adopt a defensive stance and shut down, or we can listen, acknowledge our mistake, and correct ourselves.

It can be difficult to decenter our emotions and avoid taking a defensive stance when someone points out behaviors that cause harm to others. We have all felt the sting of this type of criticism, and it can seem easier to run away from a situation than to correct ourselves and move on. It can also be embarrassing to be called out for behaviors that unintentionally cause harm to others. But as cisgender people, we need to understand that we do not have a lived experience of being trans or nonbinary, and that we need to listen and learn from others if we want to be true allies and actively participate in creating a more gender-friendly world.

It is easy to understand how a situation like the one described above may have happened; perhaps the lead teacher had not remembered to update the roster with the student's new name, or maybe it was an honest mistake on the part of the graduate student. After listening to his story, I asked him a few questions: "Why do you think the student was upset when you used her deadname? Do you think this may not be the first time the student was misgendered? Might she feel constant anxiety that someone may misgender her, or constantly be on guard in case her deadname is used by new teachers or substitutes? What do you think would have happened if you had reacted by thanking the student for correcting you and using her name correctly moving forward?"

I also shared a story about one of my research participants for my dissertation, who explained the stress he experienced on a daily basis because, "Just having to have a separate conversation about that with every single teacher you have, including substitutes—that's the worst" (quoted in Whittlesey, 2019). By the end of our conversation, the graduate student appeared to be less frustrated as he reflected upon being corrected during class. Stepping outside of his own feelings about this encounter and considering the transgender student's perspective helped him to reconsider his angry response and reframe the context of the interaction.

For those of us who benefit from cisgender privilege, it may be uncomfortable when our understanding of the world is challenged, or if one is asked to consider things like how gender is enacted upon people or how we or others perform gender. But all of us need to dive into thinking about these issues if we are to consider how to dismantle structures that prevent liberation for some of us.

It is also important to understand that just because someone corrects you (for example, if you forget to use someone's pronoun correctly or make an incorrect assumption about their gender), it does not equate to being criticized. As Julian shared with me:

Sometimes people are like, "Oh, it's really hard, but I'm going to try (to use your new name)." And it feels like they're not trying. It's really frustrating because if you call them out on it, they get upset. And it's just like, "I'm not asking a lot of you: if you misgender a dog, you correct yourself. Why can't you do that if you misgender me?" It feels like you're asking a lot of them when it really shouldn't be that way.

Adopting a growth mindset can be helpful in pushing back against feelings of defensiveness. If you are reminded about someone's pronouns in meetings with other cisgender people or asked to adjust your language or actions by trans and nonbinary community members, you should keep in mind that you cannot be expected to know everything, and that you can learn and grow from these types of interactions.

Everybody Makes Mistakes

If you mess up, I'm expecting you to mess up. I totally understand. I just want you to try.—Julian

Mistakes happen! No one expects you to be perfect. Just because you slip up and forget to use someone's pronoun correctly does not mean you are a bad person. The key is to correct yourself and move on. While you may feel horrible when this happens, it is not the time to fall over yourself apologizing; this may result in the trans or nonbinary person feeling pressure to comfort you or tell you that it's okay (when they may not feel like it was okay at all).

Chris discussed this point with me in a conversation about ineffective approaches to allyship:

> *Apologizing for misgendering to force absolution rather than to express sincere regret [causes harm]…Apologizing numerous times until you get the response you want, apologizing publicly, demanding time and resolution immediately, etc.…arguably, I would say the last instance is not an ally as they are centering themselves in my harm, but the people who do these things often self-identify as an ally.*

Once again, if you make a mistake, correct yourself and move on. Perhaps you will have time later to reflect and learn from the encounter, but putting pressure on the trans person you just misgendered to make you feel better is not appropriate. The following scene demonstrates an example of what one should not do after accidentally misgendering someone:

Server: Hi there, ladies! Welcome to XYZ Restaurant. What can I get for you today?

Sam: Actually, I'm not a lady but I'll have a soda water.

Server: Oh my gosh! I'm so sorry. I had no idea! You just look like a woman to me but it was just a mistake! I would never do that on purpose. I feel horrible!

In this scenario, the server centers their own feelings of embarrassment and guilt about making an incorrect assumption about someone's gender. Rather than briefly apologizing and moving on ("Sorry about that! I probably shouldn't assume. What can I get for you?"), the server's actions create an even more awkward situation. This is doubly harmful, as the person who was just misgendered may feel pressure to publicly forgive or brush off the event.

Being overly defensive or making a big deal about mistakes are two ways that cis people can inadvertently or unintentionally center themselves in situations that are "not about them." Performative allyship is another unhelpful approach that does not result in creating environments that acknowledge and affirm gender diversity.

Performative "Allyship"

Being a true ally is not about trying to look good in the eyes of other people or proclaiming one's support of trans and nonbinary folks to promote oneself without exerting the effort required to make positive changes for community members. Unfortunately, this type of performative "allyship"—actions that are based more in performance and virtue signaling than in equity efforts—happen frequently.

Kalina writes about this phenomenon in regard to racial equity:

> Performative allyship refers to someone from a non-marginalized group professing support and solidarity with a marginalized group, but in a way that is not helpful. Worse yet, the allyship is done in a way that may actually be harmful to "the cause." The "ally" is motivated by some type of reward. On social media, that reward is a virtual pat on the back for being a *good person* or for being *on the right side* of a cause, or *on the right side of history*… In essence, it is a show. (Kalina, 2020)

Several participants in my research spoke on this theme:

> *I come across people like this all the time, who want, like, brownie points—I call it queer points. Like, the people who are like, "Oh my god, I LOVE (LGBTQ) people, like*

my best friend is gay and I think gay people are just so great."—Frankie

The second [biggest way allyship is done ineffectively] for me is making a really big deal about my identity. For instance...[focusing on my identity in] every conversation after I come out to be about my identity (talking about nothing else).—Chris

It was really common for teachers to like, over-emphasize that they supported me, and I was like, "Are you doing this because you genuinely want to, or because you want to feel like you're, like, above everybody else?" I always felt like I was having to tell teachers it was okay to treat me like everybody else.—Charles

A key to avoiding performative allyship is to listen to the voices of the people you are trying to support and consistently engage in efforts based on their expressed needs. This approach was highlighted in the story of allyship earlier in the chapter. Julian talked about how in several cases, the members of The Melodies corrected people on his behalf when he was misgendered or when judges assumed that everyone in the group identified as female. As Shawna describes it, "We never pushed it, but we didn't hesitate to correct people." Members of the group took some of this burden away from Julian, but did not center themselves in the work or start a hashtag on social media.

They simply clarified that not all members of the group were female.

The members of The Melodies modeled allyship in these types of situations, and highlighted the importance of avoiding making assumptions at the competitions they attended. Leading by example is important if we are to make positive changes in our communities and lead to more inclusive and equitable environments for transgender and nonbinary folks.

Lead by Example

As discussed earlier, being an ally is more than using language appropriately. Cisgender people have a responsibility to actively engage in work to support more gender-friendly communities, rather than just providing polite support. This means holding other cisgender people accountable when they engage in transphobic behaviors, whether intentional or not.

As Chris says:

I think that as accomplices for whichever marginalized community we're in community with, we need to be observant and willing to act whenever we hear about or find injustice. That will mean our roller derby leagues, our workplaces, our favorite hangouts, with our families, and everywhere in between. We need to recognize that affirming pronouns is the minimum and we need to be ready to disrupt systems that oppress. Otherwise, we're reducing our responsibility to interpersonal communications and the systems that harm will stay intact.

The true ally leads by example, setting expectations and speaking out when encountering transphobic comments and behaviors.

Open the Door to Conversations

Earlier in this chapter, Julian praised his Music Director for leading by example and setting expectations for becoming a more inclusive ensemble:

The Music Director set the tone of the discussion and made it clear that the question was not, "DO we change branding?" but "HOW do we change?"

Rather than avoid the topic of gender in this originally "all-female" branded group, opening the door to this conversation (after checking with Julian) invited the other members of the group to actively participate in equity work in their ensemble, and the members of the group responded positively as a result.

You don't have to be the director of a musical ensemble to be an ally. You can set expectations within your work organizations, communities, or families and have conversations supporting more inclusive communities. Here are some examples:

- If your local cafe has two single-stall restrooms that are labeled "men" and "women," there is no harm in asking the manager why this practice is in place and requesting that the single-stall rooms be relabeled as "guest restrooms." This benefits all customers, not only transgender and nonbinary folks, as it offers more options for parents who may require baby changing areas and cuts down on lines outside restrooms.

- Many of us regularly participate in Zoom calls and other video platform calls for work and social opportunities. Why not add your pronouns next to your name in these circumstances? Adding your pronouns communicates that you acknowledge that gender diversity exists, and that we need to avoid making assumptions about gender based on how someone looks or sounds. If someone asks why you have added your pronouns, that's great! This creates dialogue about the subject and may encourage them to do the same.

- Does your local library offer books by transgender and nonbinary authors, or provide lists of books by trans authors? If not, request that the library acquires some! If necessary, share a resource with the librarians such as the "Books by Trans and Non-Binary

Authors" list by the King Country Library in Washington,[4] and see what changes might be effected.

Leading by example involves working to educate ourselves and making efforts based on what we learn. This is not always easy, especially when we encounter people who are transphobic.

Speak Out Against Transphobia

Unlike other phobias such as aquaphobia (fear of water) or acrophobia (fear of heights), transphobia is not categorized as a phobia by clinical psychology. Rather, transphobia is the hatred and distrust of transgender and/or gender non-conforming people by cisgender people. This can manifest itself in many ways. Sometimes, it may involve irrational fear or misunderstanding about trans and non-binary people, or a belief that trans identities are invalid.

Transphobia can be overt, or it may be subversive, but it can make life extremely challenging, and sometimes downright dangerous, for trans and nonbinary individuals. In my educational research, every participant shared that they had been hurt by transphobic comments or behaviors at home, school, or work. Charles shared the following story:

---

4   https://kcls.bibliocommons.com/list/share/308506797/1543470899

I was so afraid of my class, they would play "Dude (Looks Like a Lady)" every time I walked in, and they would throw down my backpack and throw paper at me and call me Caitlyn Jenner and my teacher would laugh, and then when I would say something, he'd say, "Well that's just guys just like, messin' around, and you're one of the guys now, right?"

This example is obviously extremely upsetting, in that an adult charged with protecting his students was engaging in overt transphobic behavior and not stepping in, or even encouraging, when other students were bullying Charles based on his gender. Transphobia can also be subversive, but the message continues to be clear for the target of the comment or behavior. Frankie told me about a woman at his workplace who constantly called attention to his gender, saying, "It's hidden beneath the surface":

[One time] I was carrying the ice from the ice room, they're pretty heavy but I can carry them… I lifted it up on the counter so she could put it in and she was like, "Oh my God, you're manlier than I am!" and I was like, "Did you just say that?" I looked at her and I went, "Yeah. That's cause I'm a man."

Then she wanted me to meet her boyfriend because her boyfriend found out she had been talking to a boy (me) and he was jealous …So she said to me, "Do you think you can just meet my boyfriend? I just want you to meet him 'cause he's feeling a certain kind of way—he's just the jealous type,

I just need him to meet you."Which was like, you know?
She needs him to meet me so he can see that I'm not "a real
guy"—like I'm so undesirable that she would never—she
would never date a trans person.

Frankie was acutely aware of his co-worker's demeaning
attitude regarding his gender, which made work an environment riddled with frustration and discomfort. Charles'
and Frankie's reactions to these types of interactions
demonstrate that regardless of whether transphobic comments or behaviors are enacted in undisguised or more
insidious ways, they cause harm to the individual on the
receiving end.

On a larger scale, transphobia also results in systemic
oppression of trans and nonbinary folks, as they often
experience greater challenges when seeking health care,
housing, loans, or employment (James *et al.,* 2016)—there
is even a "LGBTQ+ 'Panic' Defense" that exists in most
states in the U.S., defined as, "a legal strategy which asks
a jury to find that a victim's sexual orientation or gender
identity is to blame for the defendant's violent reaction,
including murder" (The National LGBT Bar Association,
2019). Considering that widespread transphobia is so
harmful to trans and nonbinary individuals, it is up to all
of us to stand up to transphobia wherever we encounter
it if we are to create positive changes in our communities.

Often, all it takes to reduce transphobic beliefs is
becoming more educated about gender diversity (Flores,
2015), so it is important to use opportunities in our lives

to support the people around us in learning more and to interrupt discourse based on ignorance. If you encounter situations where cisgender people speak or act in transphobic ways, don't ignore it. Instead, have a conversation about the validity of gender diversity and the need to be supportive of our trans and nonbinary friends, colleagues, and community members.

How we interrupt transphobic dialogue looks different depending on the specifics of the situation and what is said, but the most important thing is to not "let it go" when we hear it, even if it takes us out of our comfort zones. This can be challenging, but it is necessary. For example:

Uncle Ted: So your cousin Bill is "identifying" as a "she" now, whatever that means. Since I guess we can do whatever we want, I'm going to identify as a kitchen table!

Ally: Uncle Ted, I know this might be new for you and you're trying to be funny, but imagine how hurt Bella would be if she heard you talk like that. We all need to use her name properly, so please call her Bella. And I'm learning all kinds of information about what it means to be transgender and how to support trans people—if you like, I'm happy to talk about this with you and share some resources I've found that might be helpful!

Will Uncle Ted have a change of heart and begin striving towards allyship with Bella and other trans people as a result of this type of interaction? Maybe, maybe not.

But at least he will understand that those types of transphobic comments are not acceptable, even if Bella is not within earshot.

Consistently engaging when we hear transphobic comments, whether at work, with family, or in the company of friends, will make a big difference in creating more gender-friendly spaces where we live, work, and play.

Transphobia: The TERF

We all make judgments based on our biases. It's human nature. Often, we make determinations about others in a wholly unconscious way. These judgments are not informed by fact, but by our own fears or misunderstandings.

In my work as a collaborator on creating gender-friendly schools, I'm sometimes told stories or hear comments that are rooted in bias and a lack of understanding. Often, the people making these statements claim to support trans people, but with caveats. They may suggest that transgender women should not have the same rights or access to spaces that cisgender women do because sharing a restroom with a trans woman could be dangerous. This mindset does not exist in a vacuum. It pervades our culture. Perhaps you've seen news stories about celebrities who conjure up such fears, but their arguments quickly fall apart. Why? Because their assertions are false, and they do great damage because this framework reinforces the idea of "biological determinism."

Those who believe in biological determinism assert that gender is based solely on our biology. Within this framework, it is argued that trans women are not women, and trans people assigned male at birth constitute an innate threat to cisgender women. People who make these claims are often called "TERFs," which is an acronym that stands for "Trans-Exclusionary Radical Feminist."

Here are some TERF-ey comments that people have said to me, and my responses to them:

"Trans people shouldn't be able to use women's locker rooms. They might be attracted to the women who are changing."

First, gender and sexuality are two different things. A trans woman is not necessarily attracted to women or men. Second, this statement assumes that all cisgender women who use women's locker rooms are not attracted to women, which is not true. Finally, we all use locker rooms for the same thing: to shower and change. There is no need to sexualize this process.

"Women can't be safe if *men* are using the restrooms with them."

Cisgender men are typically (at least in most multi-stall restrooms in the U.S.) not using multi-stall "women's" restrooms. *Trans women* should have the option of using women's restrooms if that is where they feel safest. Although some conservative groups have pushed a narrative that trans women are a threat to cisgender women in sex-separated facilities, research data indicate otherwise, namely that it is transgender people who are much more likely to be victims of violence in these settings (Barnett, Nesbit, & Sorrentino, 2018). Concurrently, the idea that giving transgender women access to "women's rest rooms" is going to result in cisgender men dressing like women in order to perpetrate a sexual crime is also not substantiated by data.

Furthermore, it's not just transgender people who are victimized or made to feel uncomfortable in bathroom settings; cisgender people who do not fit into traditional gender stereotypes or who have a "typical" feminine/masculine body type or expression are often harassed in public restrooms. Understanding and reinforcing for others that we can't assume someone's gender by looking at them is important.

"Why was this [single-stall, locking] women's rest room turned into a gender-neutral bathroom? Can't I have a place that's just for me?"

Yes. It is a single-stall, locking bathroom that affords privacy for the one person who uses it at a time. So it's "just for you" when you are using it. Just please lock the door and wash your hands.

"Trans women should not be allowed to play on women's sports teams."

This comment is troubling, as it assumes that people assigned male at birth will always be better at every sport than those assigned female at birth, which a) is sexist and inaccurate, and b) disregards the significant variances in body types that offer certain people of all genders advantages in sports. Creating restrictions like these only serves to reinforce the concept of a fixed nature of the gender binary, and also limits educational and funding opportunities for transgender students and athletes. A number of elite athletes understand this and have spoken out against discriminatory legislation in this area: Billie Jean King, Megan Rapinoe, Layshia Clarendon, and many others have advocated for the inclusion of trans athletes on teams and competitive sports platforms that align with their gender identity. There is no reason that trans people should be excluded from playing on sports teams that align with their gender identity.

★ ★ ★

Statements like these highlight a lack of inclusiveness with regard to feminism. This mindset is limiting. The people making these statements may believe they are speaking out in concern for women's safety, but these ideas are rooted in racism, classism, and an attempt to control women's bodies—and there is simply no evidence that protecting trans women from discrimination harms cis women (Pearce, Erikainen, & Vincent, 2020).

An inclusive, intersectional approach to supporting each other in our communities has so much more potential to create safe and equitable landscapes. For example, remember how the "all-female" music group shifted to embrace Julian, who came out first as nonbinary and then as a trans man:

> *One of the things we talked about was our repertoire, because one of the songs in our repertoire was "Natural Woman." And so he said, "I'm still comfortable singing the song because I'm also all about female empowerment, even though I don't identify as female."—Shawna*

Not being a woman did not exclude Julian from celebrating femininity, just as his existence in the vocal ensemble did not threaten the femininity of the other members.

The message is clear: liberation of trans people is inherently linked with liberation for cis women (Carrera-Fernandez & DePalma, 2020; Koyama, 2003). No matter our gender, race, or sexuality, we must consider our own biases and overcome them to support one another. Doing so will enrich our lives and reduce divisions in our communities.

Actively considering how our biases impact the way we see and interact with the world is key in acknowledging and celebrating each other's humanity. Gender is only one of the elements that make up who we are. Now let's consider how different components of our identities in addition to our gender layer upon one another to impact how we navigate through the world.

Think Intersectionally

Intersectionality is a term that was coined by Kimberlé Crenshaw in 1989. It refers to how different elements of our identities intersect and overlap to impact how we perceive the world, and how the world perceives us (Crenshaw, 1989). Although Crenshaw's focus was primarily on race and gender and how U.S. legal systems are designed to replicate systems of power by ignoring overlapping layers of identity, some other examples of intersecting elements of identity include sexuality, class, religion, socio-economic status, physical ability, and more. As Torr and Bottoms write, "Gender distinctions always intersect with, and are shaded or even defined by, issues of...class, ethnicity, sexuality, and nationality" (2010, p.4).

If someone is trans or nonbinary, that is only one part of their identity, yet they often encounter discrimination as a result of that component of who they are. If they are also BIPOC (Black, Indigenous, and/or People of Color), they may experience greater discrimination because those two elements intersect.

The idea of intersectionality may be nebulous for some who are just becoming aware of how pervasive discrimination is in our society. But to be a true ally, one must consider how intersectionality impacts people in real life. For example, being trans and Black can result in a dual marginalization that puts them at increased risk for a host of issues (Jackson, Bailey, & Welles, 2018): data reveal that most violence enacted upon trans women is happening to Black trans women, and that Black transgender people have double the unemployment rate of other trans people. Furthermore, 41% of Black transgender people report experiencing homelessness at some point in their lives, which is more than five times the rate of the general U.S. population (Human Rights Campaign, 2018).

As Crenshaw writes, "When they enter, we all enter" (1989, p.167). We all need to work to dismantle systems that oppress if we are all going to benefit from a better world. Part of this is thinking and working proactively to create more equitable and inclusive environments.

To watch Kimberlé Crenshaw speak on intersectionality, you can watch her Ted Talk, "The Urgency of Intersectionality."[5]

Be Proactive

I think in order to be an ally, it actually means doing something. So often we hear folks say, "Oh, I'm a strong ally."

---

5   www.ted.com/talks/kimberle_crenshaw_the_urgency_of_intersectionality?utm_campaign=tedspread&utm_medium=referral&utm_source=tedcomshare

But that's not really a label that you can put on yourself. You have to ask: what are you doing? What are the actions and the steps that you're taking? Being an ally means taking small, everyday actions to disrupt the oppression or discrimination that might be occurring—or to be proactive and to prevent it from occurring.—Fernando

Even if we do not personally know anyone who is publicly living their life as a transgender or nonbinary person, we can make efforts to analyze the systems and institutions in which we navigate and consider how they can be improved to create safer, more inclusive, and more equitable environments to benefit us all.

I spoke with Fernando about this issue. They suggested that we ask ourselves the following questions:

- How are you proactive about looking at your space and saying, "How is this welcoming to folks from all gender identities?"

- Are there identifiers that might place folks into binary situations or have a cisnormativity lens or a heteronormativity lens?

- How are you removing those barriers?

In the "Open the Door to Conversations" section of this chapter, we touched upon some ways we can think about our environments and consider how we might make them more gender-inclusive. These types of actions can ultimately result in more inclusive environments, even if we believe that there are currently no transgender or nonbinary folks in our spaces.

The necessity of making these efforts becomes apparent when considering data regarding the exclusion or oppression of trans and nonbinary people in institutions such as workplaces or other organizations. For example, the Human Rights Campaign reports that 30% of transgender employees report experiencing mistreatment in the workplace because of their gender identity and expression, and the rate of unemployment among transgender people is three times higher than the general population (Human Rights Campaign, 2018). As Chris told me:

These are injustices that aren't going to be solved with individual actions to affirm. They're going to take accomplices disrupting hetero- and cisnormativity in their workplaces and developing a culture of affirmation where people can bring their whole selves to their work without fear of retribution or discrimination.

So how can we do this? Dr. Heath Fogg Davis suggests organizations perform "gender audits" to look at all of the ways organizations call biological sex into use and then examine whether the policies are necessary, and whether they are harmful (Davis, 2017). Here are some questions we can ask when considering whether our workplaces are gender-friendly:

- Do non-discrimination and employment policies include the terms "sexual orientation," "gender identity," and "gender expression," and is the non-discrimination policy posted in job postings to acquire more diverse employees (National LGBT Health Education Center, n.d.)?

- Does the workplace provide diversity training for all employees?

- Are there non-gendered facilities that are easily accessible throughout the building?

- Does the health insurance policy offer transgender-inclusive benefits?

- Is there a clear and accessible process for reporting and responding to discrimination?

- If this is a healthcare organization, is data regarding gender and sexuality gathered in an appropriate and meaningful way? (See Bradford *et al.*, 2012; National LGBT Health Education Center, n.d.; Vincent, 2017 for examples and suggestions.)

All organizations should be asking these questions, regardless of whether there are trans or nonbinary people who are "out" in the organization.

In addition, as discussed earlier in the book, we can each make a habit of sharing our pronouns in meetings, on name tags, and online to send a message that gender cannot be assumed and that gender diversity is acknowledged and accepted. Shawna, one of The Melodies from our story of trans allyship, has gotten into the habit of doing this, and tells me:

> *Just introducing myself in meetings, I now use my pronouns. I say, "I'm Shawna and I use she/her pronouns." Even if it's not a required part of our introduction, I make a point to include it because I know there are people who may not feel so comfortable sharing theirs and the more cisgender folks who do include theirs, it can make it more comfortable for trans or nonbinary people in the room.*

These approaches may take some effort, especially in dealing with organizations that have a long way to go in acknowledging and supporting gender diversity. However, they are fundamental in laying the groundwork for more inclusive and equitable communities for all of us.

CONCLUSION: THE FUTURE OF GENDER

So what would happen if we focused less on assigned sex at birth, less on gender overall, and more on embracing individuality? What if we, as Davis writes, "use the transgender experience to fundamentally question the social custom of administering sex" (2017, p.19)?

Even if some people are railing against this idea of letting go of old-fashioned expectations about gender, times are changing! Gender is increasingly acknowledged as expansive and diverse. For many "Zoomers" (those born in the late 1990s or early 2000s) and Gen Alphas (born after Gen Z), concepts of gender are more fluid, and these individuals often embrace gender diversity or accept a change of pronouns naturally without the need for deep explanation. For example, when I told my ten-year-old niece that I was writing my first book, *It's OK to Say "They"*, she asked what it was about. I could sense the other adults' ears pricking up, wondering how I would explain. However, I just asked if she knew about trans kids, and she responded with, "Oh, yeah, I know Jazz (Jennings) from YouTube. She's really pretty." My niece didn't even think about it. She automatically used the correct pronoun for Jazz (who is trans and a trans advocate), and we simply went on with the craft project we had been working on. Interactions like this and others that I have had with youth give me hope that we are moving in a more inclusive direction in regard to gender.

Furthermore, in addition to the steps outlined in the previous chapters about approaches to striving to be a true ally, what would happen if we all considered our own gender and what it means to us? What if we think about what we enjoy about our gender, and what expectations we put on ourselves because of gender? Could this help us to understand ourselves better, to more fully celebrate our own gender and others' genders? Could this help us to take some pressure off ourselves to perform gender in a particular way because of expectations others have placed upon us?

I have suggested this activity to other cisgender people, most of whom consider the suggestion thoughtfully. I have also had people respond with comments like:

Why would I have to think about that? I'm a man. I've always been a man. And that's just how it is.

I'm a woman and there's nothing more complicated

about it than that. I don't understand why I would need to do this.

However, my assertion is that reflecting upon our own gender and the expectations enacted upon us because of gender will not threaten our own cisgender status. Rather, engaging in thinking more about gender instead of running on gender autopilot can help us to learn more about ourselves and our society.

Moreover, what would happen if we were to decenter gender in what and how we consume? Why do we need "girls'" and "boys'" sections in toy stores or in clothing departments? Toys don't have innate genders, and neither do articles of clothing. Maria talked about this point with me, and how her youngest son enjoys engaging in some traditionally feminine pursuits, such as painting his nails. She says,

> *I always say to him, "Oh, people will tell you that boys don't like nail polish or can't wear nail polish. But do you know who likes nail polish? People who like nail polish!" You can decide your interests apart from your gender, or some of your interests might be gender affirming for you. And that's wonderful.*

As a result of Maria's approach, her son is comfortable exploring many types of activities and exploring his own likes and dislikes without having the burden of being told, "That's not okay because you're a boy."

Contrary to what some may believe, creating gender-friendly communities will not take anything away from cisgender folks. However, "destigmatizing, demedicalizing, and decolonizing...gender as a thing in the world" (Bergman, 2018, p.13) *will* have significant positive results for not only trans and nonbinary people, but cis people as well! More inclusive communities would clearly benefit transgender individuals, who would not be constantly required to fight to have the validity of their gender accepted—and often, fighting for survival itself—within a binary gender system. And cisgender people would benefit from less restrictive gender "rules"—if you're a cis man who likes painting his nails, you can do so without the person next to you on the bus giving you the side-eye! If you're a cis woman in Japan who enjoys the odd salty rice snack, you could enjoy it without being snickered at by cashiers!

Additionally, imagine if the barriers to housing, employment, and health care that currently exist for trans and nonbinary individuals were removed, and what ways we might all benefit from learning from more diverse perspectives and ideas! To me this sounds like a beautiful, more liberated future for all—so let's do all we can to make it come to fruition.

Reader, thank you for joining me in striving to be a true ally with our trans and nonbinary family members, friends, colleagues, and community members. Remember: this process does not end when you finish this book. It is a lifelong process. I hope you will continue to explore resources like the ones at the end of this book to learn more, and that you will work to build capacity for inclusiveness and equality wherever you live!

BOOK STUDY/ DISCUSSION QUESTIONS

- Was there anything that surprised you in the book? What resonated with you? What challenged you?

- Regardless of what your gender is, do you describe yourself as a feminist? Is your feminism intersectional? How can you tell?

- What types of expectations do you think others have had for you in regard to gender? How did/does this make you feel?

- Have you observed family, friends, or colleagues making transphobic comments? How have you reacted to this in the past? How might you react to these types of situations in the future?

- Practice introducing yourself with your name and pronoun. Are there contexts in which you may begin doing this in your work or personal life?

- Consider the spaces that you navigate in your daily life. Are they welcoming to transgender and nonbinary people? Why or why not? What can you do to be proactive and create more gender-friendly environments?

RESOURCES

This section provides a *very* small sample of resources that share stories, offer support, and present ways to further engage in striving to be true allies.

Websites

http://alokvmenon.com
Video, artwork, and writing by gender non-conforming artist, author, and activist ALOK.

http://eminism.org
Blog, presentations, readings, and more by social justice activist and writer Emi Koyama. Emi's writing engages with topics ranging from feminism to sexual and domestic violence to intersex and disability issues, among others.

http://marshap.org
Website of the Marsha P. Johnson Institute, focused on elevating and supporting the voices of Black trans people.

http://micahbazant.com
Website of internationally renowned trans visual artist Micah Bazant.

http://mypronouns.org
Website by Shige Sakurai, founder of International Pronouns Day, providing information about personal pronoun use and suggestions for how to handle mistakes.

http://pflag.org/glossary
PFLAG is an organization that supports lesbian, gay, bisexual, transgender, and queer (LGBTQ+) people, their parents and families, and allies. This page offers an extensive glossary of terminology related to LGBTQ+ folks and issues.

https://pronouns.minus18.org.au
"Pronouns" practice app that runs users through examples of how different pronouns are used in various cases.

http://straightforequality.org
Website by PFLAG designed to empower allies who don't necessarily have a personal connection to the lesbian, gay, bisexual, transgender, and queer (LGBTQ+) community.

http://talbot-heindl.com
Features writing, art, guides for workplaces, and an illustrated online zine *Chrissplains Nonbinary Advocacy to Cisgender People.*

http://transequality.org
Website of the National Center for Transgender Equality, offering wide-ranging resources for transgender and cisgender people alike.

http://translash.org
Shares stories of members of the trans community and features a blog, videos of TransLash podcasts, a database of trans-owned businesses, and more.

Podcasts

Gender Reveal with Tuck Woodstock.
Gender Stories with Alex Iantaffi.
Marsha's Plate with Diamond Stylz, Mia Mix, and Zee.
One From the Vaults with Morgan M. Page.
Queersplaining with Callie Wright.
TransLash with Imara Jones.
Transcripts with Andrea Jenkins and Myrl Beam.
What the Trans!? With Michelle O'Toole and Ashleigh Talbot.

Documentaries

A Place in the Middle
This documentary shares the story of Ho'onani, an 11-year-old girl whose dream is to lead her school's all-male hula troupe. Ho'onani is māhū (a traditional Hawaiian term describing a person who embraces both masculine and feminine traits).

Disclosure
Disclosure presents thoughtful perspectives and analysis by trans folks about Hollywood's impact on the trans community.

Mala Mala
Mala Mala focuses on the lives of three nonbinary people in Puerto Rico.

Paris Is Burning
This documentary explores stories of Black, Latinx queer and trans ballroom community members in 1980s New York City.

Passing
This award-winning film explores issues of intersectionality as it presents the experiences of three Black transgender men.

Pay It No Mind: The Life and Times of Marsha P. Johnson
This documentary tells the story of trans activist Marsha P. Johnson through her own words and interviews with those who knew her.

The Trans List
This film by Timothy Greenfield-Sanders profiles 11 transgender and nonbinary people with stories told in their own words.

Transgender, at War and in Love
Fiona Dawson's documentary presents the experiences of a trans military couple who are banned from serving openly.

Transhood
Transhood chronicles the lives of four young people and their families as they navigate growing up transgender in America's heartland. There are also accompanying resources for the documentary.[1]

Books

A Quick & Easy Guide to Queer & Trans Identities by Mady G & J. R. Zuckerberg.
Asegi Stories: Cherokee Queer and Two-Spirit Memory by Qwo-Li Driskill.
Being Jazz: My Life as A (Transgender) Teen by Jazz Jennings.
Beyond the Gender Binary by Alok Vaid-Menon.
Beyond Trans: Does Gender Matter? by Dr. Heath Fogg Davis.
Gender: Your Guide: A Gender-Friendly Primer on What to Know, What to Say, and What to Do in the New Gender Culture by Dr. Lee Airton.
Gender Trouble: Feminism and the Subversion of Identity by Judith Butler.
Gender Queer: A Memoir by Maia Kobabe.
Intersection Allies: We Make Room for All by Chelsea Johnson, LaToya Council, and Carolyn Choi, illustrated by Ashley Seil Smith.
Redefining Realness: My Path To Womanhood, Identity, Love & So Much More by Janet Mock.

---

1   www.hbo.com/documentaries/transhood/resources

Sissy: A Coming-of-Gender Story by Jacob Tobia.
Super Late Bloomer: My Early Days in Transition: An Up and Out Collection by Julia Kaye.
Surpassing Certainty: What My Twenties Taught Me by Janet Mock.
Tomorrow Will Be Different: Love, Loss, and the Fight for Trans Equality by Sarah McBride.
The Trans Allyship Workbook by Davey Shlasko.
Undoing Gender by Judith Butler.

Hashtags to Follow

#BlackTransLivesMatter
#DefendTransYouth
#GirlsLikeUs
#OKtoSayThey
#RedefiningRealness
#TransDayOfVisibility
#TransIsBeautiful
#TransLivesMatter
#TransphobiaIsASin
#TransPeopleAreDivine
#TransRightsAreHumanRights

REFERENCES

Airton, L. (2012) *They is My Pronoun.* Accessed on 3/8/2021 at www.theyismypronoun.com.

Airton, L. (2018) *Gender: Your Guide: A Gender-Friendly Primer on What to Know, What to Say, and What to Do in the New Gender Culture.* Avon, MA: Adams Media.

Annamma, S. A., Jackson D., & Morrison, D. (2017) 'Conceptualizing color-evasiveness: Using dis/ability critical race theory to expand a color-blind racial ideology in education and society.' *Race Ethnicity and Education 20,* 2, 147–162.

Anzani, A., Morris, E., & Galupo, M. (2019) 'From absence of microaggressions to seeing authentic gender: Transgender experiences with microaffirmations in therapy.' *Journal of LGBT Issues in Counseling 13,* 4, 258–275.

Barnett, B., Nesbit, A., & Sorrentino, R. (2018) 'The transgender bathroom debate at the intersection of politics, law, ethics, and science.' *Journal of the American Academy of Psychiatry and the Law Online 46,* 2, 232–241.

Bazant, M. (n.d.) About. Accessed on 3/8/2021 at www.micahbazant.com/about.

Bergman, S. B. (2018) 'Foreword.' In A. Iantaffi & M.-J. Barker *How to Understand Your Gender: A Practical Guide for Exploring Who You Are.* London: Jessica Kingsley Publishers.

Bolger, M. (2016) 'Top 5 Trans Ally Principles.' *Social Justice Toolbox.* Accessed on 3/8/2021 at www.socialjusticetoolbox.com/top-5-trans-ally-principles.

Bradford, J., Cahill, S., Grasso, C., & Makadon, H. (2012) *How to Gather Data on Sexual Orientation and Gender Identity in Clinical Settings.*

The Fenway Institute. Accessed on 3/8/2021 at https://fenwayhealth. org/wp-content/uploads/2015/09/Policy_Brief_HowtoGather..._ v3_01.09.12.pdf.

Bryant-Jefferies, R. (2004) *Models of Care for Drug Service Provision.* San Francisco, CA: Radcliffe.

Butler, J. (1988) 'Performative acts and gender constitution: An essay in phenomenology and feminist theory.' *Theatre Journal 40*, 4, 519–531.

Carrera-Fernandez, M. V. & DePalma, R. (2020) 'Feminism will be trans-inclusive or it will not be: Why do two cis-hetero woman educators support transfeminism?' *The Sociological Review 68*, 4, 745–762.

Cava, P. (2016) 'Cisgender and Cissexual.' In N. Naples (Ed.) *The Wiley-Blackwell Encyclopedia of Gender and Sexuality Studies.* Hoboken, NJ: John Wiley & Sons.

Chang, T. K. & Chung, Y. B. (2015) 'Transgender microaggressions: Complexity of the heterogeneity of transgender identities.' *Journal of LGBT Issues in Counseling 9*, 3, 217–234.

Crenshaw, K. (1989) 'Demarginalizing the intersection of race and sex: A Black feminist critique of antidiscrimination doctrine, feminist theory and antiracist politics.' *University of Chicago Legal Forum 1989*, 1. Accessed on 3/8/2021 at http://chicagounbound.uchicago.edu/uclf/vol1989/iss1/8.

Davis, H. F. (2017) *Beyond Trans: Does Gender Matter?* New York: New York University Press.

Deblinger, E., Mannarino, A., Cohen, J., Runyon, M., & Heflin, A. H. (2015) *Child Sexual Abuse: A Primer for Treating Children, Adolescents, and their Nonoffending Parents.* New York: Oxford University Press.

Flanders, C. F. (2015) 'Bisexual health: A daily diary analysis of stress and anxiety.' *Basic and Applied Social Psychology 37*, 6, 319–335.

Flores, A. R. (2015) 'Attitudes toward transgender rights: Perceived knowledge and secondary interpersonal contact.' *Politics, Groups, and Identities 3*, 3, 398–416.

Gender Census (2020) *2013–2020 Popularity Over Time.* Accessed on 3/29/2021 at https://gendercensus.com/results/2019-worldwide.

Green, E., Benner, K., & Pear, R. (2018) '"Transgender" could be defined out of existence under Trump administration.' *The New York Times.* Accessed on 3/8/2021 at www.nytimes.com/2018/10/21/us/politics/transgender-trump-administration-sex-definition.html.

Human Rights Campaign (2018) *Dismantling a Culture of Violence: Understanding Anti-Transgender Violence and Ending the Crisis.*

Accessed on 3/8/2021 at https://assets2.hrc.org/files/assets/resources/2018AntiTransViolenceReportSHORTENED.pdf?_ga=2.124176526.528288488.1592062648-817983976.1592062648.

Human Rights Campaign (2020) *Fatal Violence Against the Transgender and Gender Non-Conforming Community in 2020.* Accessed on 4/30/2021 at www.hrc.org/resources/violence-against-the-trans-and-gender-non-conforming-community-in-2020.

Jackson, S., Bailey, M., & Welles, B. F. (2018) '#GirlsLikeUs: Trans advocacy and community building online.' *New Media & Society 20,* 5, 1868–1888.

James, S. E., Herman, J. L., Rankin, S., Keisling, M., Mottet, M., & Anafi, M. (2016) *The Report of the 2015 U.S. Transgender Survey.* Washington, DC: National Center for Transgender Equality.

Kahn, E., Johnson, A., Lee, M., & Miranda, L. (2018) *2018 LGBTQ Youth Report.* Human Rights Campaign Foundation Public Education & Research Program. Accessed on 3/8/2021 at https://assets2.hrc.org/files/assets/resources/2018-YouthReport-0514-Final.pdf .

Kalina, P. (2020) 'Performative Allyship.' *Technium Social Sciences Journal, Technium Science 11,* 1, 478–481.

Killermann, S. (2011) '30+ examples of cisgender privilege.' *It's Pronounced Metrosexual.* Accessed on 3/8/2021 at http://itspronouncedmetrosexual.com/2011/11/list-of-cisgender-privileges.

Koch, J. M., Knutson, D., Loche, L., Loche III, R. W., Lee, H.-S., & Federici, D. J. (2020) 'A qualitative inquiry of microaffirmation experiences among culturally diverse graduate students.' *Current Psychology: A Journal for Diverse Perspectives on Diverse Psychological Issues.* Accessed on 4/30/2021 at https://doi.org/10.1007/s12144-020-00811-3.

Koyama, E. (2003) 'The transfeminist manifesto.' In R. Dicker & A. Piepmeier (Eds) *Catching a Wave: Reclaiming Feminism for the Twenty-First Century* (pp.244–259). Boston, MA: Northeastern University Press.

Kraehe, A. & Brown, K. (2011) 'Awakening teachers' capacities for social justice with/in arts-based inquiries.' *Equity & Excellence in Education 44,* 4, 488–511.

Leonardo, Z. & Porter, R. (2010) 'Pedagogy of fear: Toward a Fanonian theory of "safety" in race dialogue.' *Race Ethnicity and Education 13,* 2, 139–157.

Mandela, N. (1995) *Long Walk to Freedom: The Autobiography of Nelson Mandela.* Boston, MA: Back Bay Books.

Merriam-Webster (2019) 'They' Is Merriam-Webster's Word of the Year 2019. Accessed on 3/8/2021 at www.merriam-webster.com/words-at-play/woty2019-top-looked-up-words-they.

The National LGBT Bar Association (2019) *LGBTQ+ "Panic" Defense.* Accessed on 3/8/2021 at http://lgbtbar.org/programs/advocacy/gay-trans-panic-defense.

National LGBT Health Education Center (n.d.) *Focus on Forms and Policy: Creating an Inclusive Environment for LGBT patients.* Accessed on 3/8/2021 at www.lgbtqiahealtheducation.org/wp-content/uploads/2017/08/Forms-and-Policy-Brief.pdf.

Nealy, E. (2017) *Transgender Children and Youth: Cultivating Pride and Joy with Families in Transition.* New York: W.W. Norton & Company.

Needham, B. L. & Austin, E. L. (2010) 'Sexual orientation, parental support, and health during the transition to young adulthood.' *Journal of Youth and Adolescence 39*, 1189–1198.

Pearce, R., Erikainen, S., & Vincent, B. (2020) 'TERF wars: An introduction.' *The Sociological Review 68*, 4, 677–698.

Phillips, M. (2017) 'Trump administration rescinds guidance on transgender rights under Title IX.' *JacksonLewis.* Accessed on 3/29/21 at www.jacksonlewis.com/publication/trump-administration-rescinds-guidance-transgender-rights-under-title-ix.

Pollock, K. (2018) 'Cis is not a slur.' *The Queerness.* Accessed on 3/8/2021 at https://thequeerness.com/2018/02/23/cis-is-not-a-slur.

Powell, C., Demetriou, C., & Fisher, A. (2013) 'Micro-affirmations in academic advising: Small acts, big impact.' *The Mentor: An Academic Advising Journal.* Accessed on 3/29/2021 https://journals.psu.edu/mentor/article/view/61286/60919.

Pulice-Farrow, L., Bravo, A. P., & Galupo, M. P. (2019) '"Your gender is valid": Microaffirmations in the romantic relationships of transgender individuals.' *Journal of LGBT Issues in Counseling 13*, 1.

Pulice-Farrow, L., Clements, Z. A., & Galupo, M. P. (2017) 'Patterns of transgender micro-aggressions in friendship: The role of gender identity.' *Psychology & Sexuality 8*, 3, 189–207.

Reidel, S. (2017) 'Deadnaming a trans person is violence – So why does the media do it anyway?' *Medium.* Accessed on 3/29/2021 at https://medium.com/the-establishment/deadnaming-a-trans-person-is-violence-so-why-does-the-media-do-it-anyway-19500eda4b4.

Ryan, C., Russell, S. T., Huebner, D., Diaz, R., & Sanchez, J. (2010)

'Family acceptance in adolescence and the health of LGBT young adults.' *Journal of Child and Adolescent Psychiatric Nursing 23*, 205–213.

Tarca, K. (2005) 'Colorblind in control: The risks of resisting difference amid demographic change.' *Educational Studies 38*, 2, 99–120.

Thein, A. (2013) 'Language arts teachers' resistance to teaching LGBT literature and issues.' *Language Arts 90*, 3, 169–180.

Torr, D. & Bottoms, S. (2010) *Sex, Drag, and Male Roles: Investigating gender as Performance.* Ann Arbor, MI: University of Michigan Press.

The Trevor Project (2019) *National Survey on LGBTQ Mental Health.* New York: The Trevor Project.

The United States Department of Justice (2017) 'Attorney General Sessions issues guidance on federal law protections for religious liberty.' Justice News. Accessed on 3/8/2021 at www.justice.gov/opa/pr/attorney-general-sessions-issues-guidance-federal-law-protections-religious-liberty.

TransLash (n.d.) About Us. Accessed on 3/8/2021 at https://translash.org/about.

Vincent, B. (2017) 'I am your trans patient.' *BMJ, 357*, j2963. Accessed on 3/8/2021 at https://doi.org/10.1136/bmj.j2963.

Whittlesey, C. (2019) 'Translations: Exploring and sharing experiences of transgender and non-binary students.' Unpublished doctoral dissertation, University of Massachusetts Lowell.

Wu, J. (2015) '"On this side": The production, progression, and potential of cisgender.' Unpublished thesis, Dept. of Linguistics, Swarthmore College.

INDEX